TWENTY-SEVENTH CERAMIC NATIONAL EXHIBITION

EVERSON MUSEUM OF ART

TWENTY-SEVENTH CERAMIC NATIONAL EXHIBITION

AMERICAN CERAMICS NOW

SYRACUSE NEW YORK ▲ 1987

This publication was prepared on the occasion of the exhibition
AMERICAN CERAMICS NOW: The 27th Ceramic National Exhibition.

ISBN: 0-914407-08-2

Library of Congress Catalogue Number: 87-080542

Everson Museum of Art is supported by the New York State Council on the Arts, Onondaga County, the City of Syracuse, National Endowment for the Arts, membership, independent contributions, and endowments.

AMERICAN CERAMICS NOW: The 27th Ceramic National Exhibition has been made possible in part with public funds from the New York State Council on the Arts.

Additional funding has come from B.G. Sulzle, Inc., Mr. and Mrs. Alfred J. Flanagan, Mrs. H.G. Sulzle, Mr. Daniel J. Murphy, and Pass & Seymour, Inc.—A member of the Legrand Group.

Editor: Thomas Piché Jr.

Design: C. W. Pike

Photography:
Courtney Frisse
(Karen Meyers, p. 48
eeva-inkeri, pp. 14, 28)

Typesetting:
Dupli Graphics
Typographers
in ITC Avant Garde Gothic

Printing: Salina Press
in an edition of 5,000

EXHIBITION SCHEDULE

EVERSON MUSEUM OF ART, Syracuse, NY
April 8–June 28, 1987

AMERICAN CRAFT MUSEUM, New York, NY
July 31–October 18, 1987

CROCKER ART MUSEUM, Sacramento, CA
November 21–December 27, 1987

DE CORDOVA AND DANA MUSEUM AND PARK, Lincoln, MA
January 14–March 12, 1989

BUTLER INSTITUTE OF ART, Youngstown, OH
April 12–May 24, 1989

SHELDON MEMORIAL ART GALLERY, UNIVERSITY OF NEBRASKA—LINCOLN,
Lincoln, NE
June 15–August 15, 1989

BIRMINGHAM MUSEUM OF ART, Birmingham, AL
September 6–November 15, 1989

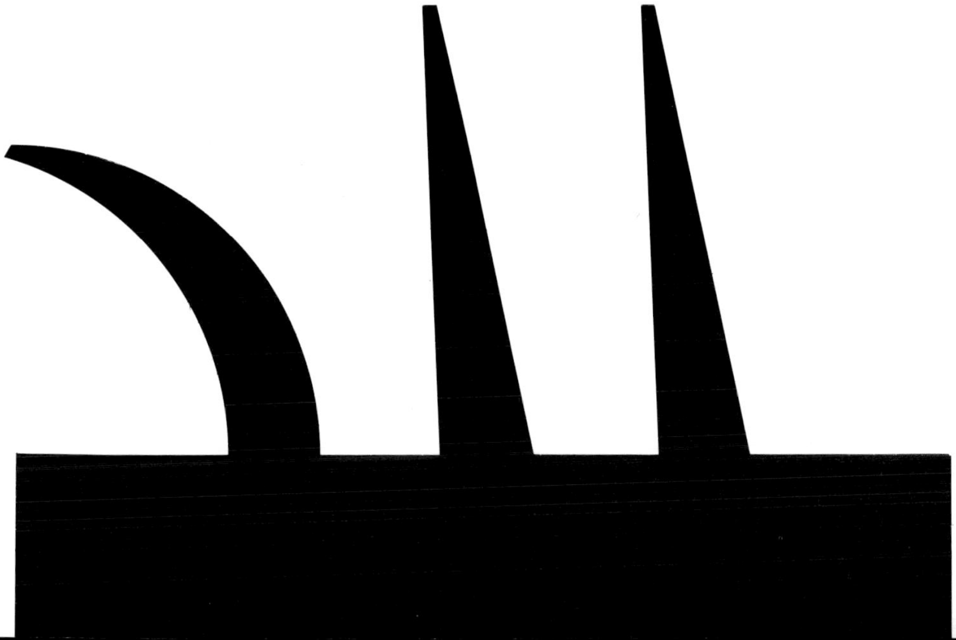

The organization of an exhibition such as this one requires the cooperation of many people. Everson Museum is particularly grateful to the New York State Council on the Arts for its generous support, and to Dorothy and Robert Riester and The Hancock Foundation for funding the purchase prizes.

The judges and advisory board performed their duties with sensitivity and discretion, and to them we are indebted for assembling such a thoroughly representative exhibition.

The Museum is particularly grateful for the help of the following galleries: Rena Bransten Gallery, CDS Gallery, Garth Clark Gallery, Charles Cowles Gallery, Helen Drutt Gallery, Allan Frumkin Gallery, Wanda Hansen Gallery, Theo Portnoy Gallery, Max Protetch Gallery, Esther Saks Gallery, and Bernice Steinbaum Gallery, and the Fred and Estelle Marer Collection at Scripps College, Claremont, California.

We also wish to thank the artists who cooperated so cheerfully to see that their work arrived on time.

Greg Daley and Courtney Frisse handled the installation and the photography like the professionals they are, and with great patience. C. W. Pike has produced a uniquely creative theme for the catalogue that employs motifs based on the firing of ceramics: cones, heat waves, and the spyhole. A hearty round of applause must also go to the Everson staff: to Tom Piché, public information officer, for preparing the catalogue and publicity; Registrar John Rexine for his attention to crating, shipping, and installation details; Carole Burke, office manager, for creating and keeping order; and especially to Gussie Will Alex, Manuel Burgos, and Rapha Johnson for being there every time they were needed for things both large and small.

Barbara Perry

INTRODUCTION

The idea of reinstating the *Ceramic National Exhibition* at the Everson has admittedly been long in the making. Without any particular pressure, it seemed good timing for the Museum to organize a contemporary survey of American ceramics now. A hiatus of fifteen years between this show and the last has given the Everson time to consolidate and extend its own collections, build its facilities and staff, study the past, contribute to the history of ceramics in a number of groundbreaking exhibitions and publications, and thereafter reassess its commitment to the medium.

During this same time, the art world has grown enormously, and recognition of ceramics as a vital art form has made considerable progress. The question as to whether or not there still remains a need for a national juried exhibition of ceramics is, in fact, more arguable today than it was in the 1960s, and certainly more arguable than when the *Ceramic National* began in Syracuse in 1932.

Today there is a growing critical audience for ceramics, as evidenced by the flourishing of such national journals as *American Ceramics, American Crafts,* and *Ceramics Monthly.* Also, more and more art galleries of prestige include ceramists in their stables, and a number of galleries are devoted exclusively to ceramics; the ceramists they represent command increasingly respectable prices for their work. These galleries have reached sophisticated standards of quality and have won respect on the national art scene. Indeed, it is a far cry today from the situation of the early seventies when crafts fairs, craft shops, an occasional university gallery show, or a general design exhibition were the only places likely for sales and exposure for the ceramist.

While much has transpired in a positive way during the past fifteen years, heightening the self-esteem of the ceramist and educating the public as to the aeshetic value of ceramics, there obviously remains much more to be accomplished. This is particularly so in the field of education. There remains an appalling lack of knowledge about the history and tradition of ceramics, especially as compared to scholarship in the fields of painting and sculpture. Major museums and major exhibitions that review contemporary art, as often as not, still regularly omit any objects by artists working in clay. Just as painting has its own history, ceramics, too, is an art form with a history and aesthetic criteria and connoisseurship of its own. (A notable difference between the two is that ceramics is a more universal art form.) The history of ceramics has yet to be explored by professors of art, critics, curators, or even artist/teachers. More extensive education and greater exposure on the levels of the university and the museum seem necessary in order to achieve a wider and more mature level of appreciation for the art of ceramics.

In organizing this exhibition we became aware that no other museum or gallery in the county has ever quite filled the void left since the last *Ceramic National* was mounted in Syracuse in 1972. There arose no other wide-ranging periodical review of American ceramics on the level of the biannual retrospective of contemporary American art at the Whitney Museum, or of international art at the Carnegie Art Museum in Pittsburgh. Even though reputable art dealers now regularly do show ceramics, which are presented as professionally as any other art form, commercial art galleries inevitably have their limitations. There are space and scheduling restrictions, and limited resources for discovering emerging clay artists. What is shown is often limited by what sells, which involves the tastes of the dealers and their clients, and even the size of the works shown.

In the final analysis, then, the Everson's *Ceramic National Exhibition* still serves a unique purpose: to assemble from as wide-ranging a national constituency as possible a large exhibition of works that best distinguish the clay art of our times. Without particular regard to previous reputation or vested interests, the works were selected because the juror-curators were unabashedly impressed with their presence—idealistic of course, but very much in line with the ideas that inspired the original exhibitions in the 1930s.

The first part of the *27th Ceramic National Exhibition* is a survey of artists selected by an advisory board made up of twenty-five knowledgeable artists, teachers, critics, and curators. Their nominations were compiled and on the basis of their recommendations nineteen artists were invited to participate, artists whose work has been widely recognized and has received outstanding critical response over the past decade.

The other component of the exhibition, and that for which it was originally instituted, consists of works by artists who are less well-known. Their work was reviewed by three judges in whose estimation qualities of achievement had been reached that qualified them for inclusion. The judges themselves were engaged due to a combination of their own identifiable virtues: breadth of knowledge of contemporary art in general, depth and discriminating knowledge in the field of ceramics per se, and their representation of good geographic distribution. So, cultivated yet differing perspectives, keen insights into the innovative possibilities of the medium of clay, and a set of erudite eyes, seasoned by years of passionate "looking," combined to select this outstanding presentation of contemporary ceramics.

We are delighted to open the exhibition in Syracuse with the accompanying attendance of the members of the National Council on Education for the Ceramic Arts. We are hopeful that the anticipated reception given to the show by this group will be followed by an equally appreciative national audience as the exhibition travels to other locales around the country during its two-year tour.

The evolution and evaluation of ceramics continues and probably will as long as there is clay and as long as there is genius to give it shape and ideational substance. It is hoped that the *27th Ceramic National* will be seen as furthering the spiral toward the apotheosis of contemporary clay art.

RONALD A. KUCHTA
Director, Everson Museum of Art

Barbara Haskell

Curator, Whitney Museum of American Art, New York, NY

Henry Hopkins

Director, Frederick R. Weisman Collection, Los Angeles, CA

Michael McTwigan

Editor, *American Ceramics*

Advisory board for invitational artists

Rena Bransten
Elena Canavier
Garth Clark
Helen W. Drutt English
Kenneth Ferguson
Henry Geldzahler
Barbara Haskell
Lloyd Herman
Wayne Higby
Henry Hopkins
Jerome Horning
Margie Hughto
Ed Lebow
Martha Lynn
David McFadden
Michael McTwigan
Jim Melchert
Eudora Moore
John Perreault
Susan Peterson
Betty Sheinbaum
Rose Slivka
Paul Smith
Judith Schwartz
Alice Westphal

Adelaide Robineau would be pleased. It was to her, the doyenne of American ceramics, that the *Ceramic National Exhibitions* were originally dedicated. It was Robineau's exquisite porcelains that became the nucleus of the collection of Everson Museum. And there is, at long last, in many of these most recent works by America's finest ceramists, reiteration of the spirit and sensibility that characterize her oeuvre. This does not infer, by any means, a return to the past or even a reference to tradition. Possibly, many of these artists have never heard of Robineau. But there is a refreshing change in American ceramics, one that has been afoot for some time, but seems more manifest in this encompassing selection of work.

To better understand American ceramics now, one needs only to refer back to the last *Ceramic National* held in 1972. The early seventies saw the Expressionist and Funk movements in full bloom. There was violence, anger, and affectation. Forms were free, heavy, purposely clumsy, and gestural. Color, when it was used, was garish, direct, and candid. The spotlight was on the gutsy, "let's let it all hang out" school. Rules were broken, traditions foresaken, and institutions abandoned. All this gave American ceramics the much needed shot in the arm to bring it out of the doldrums of the last vestiges of the post-war stoneware era.

The early eighties brought a different sensibility, but one that utilized the changes initiated during the previous decade. There was a renewed interest in the vessel, and along with it, an explosion of color. Decoration was rediscovered and formalism began to creep in here and there.

THE 27TH CERAMIC NATIONAL EXHIBITION

The *27th Ceramic National* has brought together eighty-two objects that aptly illustrate both contemporary ceramics' debt to the 1960s and 70s, and a new sensibility that has formed in the last few years; one that is in keeping with recent trends found in the American art world at large. In order to provide a balanced view of contemporary American ceramics, the exhibition has been divided into two sections—invitational and juried. Together they provide a comprehensive survey of American ceramics today.

Nineteen masters chosen by a twenty-five person advisory board were to send one piece done within the past five years. The works that they have submitted serve to provide a basis for the exhibition, and illustrate the present position of some of the ceramists active at the time of the last *Ceramic National* (nine of the nineteen participated in that exhibition). Nearly all have changed with the times, but these changes are often subtle and seldom obliterate that unique quality which has imbued the work of each individual from the start. The art world today is so often caught up in innovation, in looking for something new or different, that it often overlooks the subtle nuances on an already clearly defined aesthetic, or work that simply exhibits exceptionally high quality and sensitivity. Thus, the objects in the invitational section of the exhibition offer an interesting study in both the development and the staying power of the artists' personal visions.

One is still able to recognize the work of William Daley, Wayne Higby, Rudy Autio, Paul Soldner, and Rudolf Staffel, for instance, for there has been no abrupt change of direction in their oeuvre, but rather a fuller realization and maturity of expression. Mary Frank's figures remain romantic and sensual, both in subject matter and in the way the material is used. Jun Kaneko has left behind the more expressionistic aspects of his style, but still pursues the same motifs with a greater sophistication and subtlety. Ron Nagle has turned to purely sculptural forms that still retain the preciousness and singularity of his earier cups and vessels, but that have an unusual monumentality about them in spite of their small size. John Mason has proceeded consistently and surely from his early expressionist style to one more formalist, even minimialist, and here is represented by a piece entirely indicative of his current position. Jack Earl has stretched considerably, with evocative, personal works with surreal overtones. Ken Price continues to deal with aesthetic problems, but uses innovative iconographic motifs.

The juried part of the exhibition mirrors the pluralism that characterizes the contemporary art scene. Like a great smorgasbord, there is something for everyone. Best of all, each piece has been accepted on its own merits, not because of its adherence to a prescribed formula, aesthetic, or style.

There are many pieces that continue the tactile, gestural, spontaneous characteristics of the sixties and seventies. In the work of Virginia Scotchie, Arlene Shechet, and Stanton Welsh, for instance, the medium is apparent, even emphasized, and forms are monumental but relatively unrefined. In the work of Richard Notkin there is a resurgence of social commentary, but now it is more cerebral, less abdominal and gestural, more symbolic. And there is still a certain surrealist quality to some work, such as that of Scott Chamberlin and Mark Burns.

The majority of the accepted artworks illustrate two new aspects of the current American ceramic scene. Many exhibit a tendency toward the baroque, sometimes through strangely disquieting torsion, like energy gone haywire. Forms are often agitated, twisted, full of movement, like a Bernini column—baroque, but in the broad sense of the term. The pieces of Abby Huntoon, James Lawton, and Janet Neuwalder, though smooth and crisp, undulate and twist with a spirited energy. Belinda Gabryl's *Tornado Teapot* seemingly twists out of control, and Chris Gustin's vase writhes upward.

This baroque quality does not imply disorder or an absence of clarity. Quite the opposite. By and large, forms are crisp and clean, very controlled, even when they are made to appear to be out of control. While there is often a sort of obliqueness, as in the pieces by Curtis and Suzan Benzle and Mara Superior, this is always contained, even restrained. Forms are explicit and clearly defined, though they are often restless or in motion. The untitled jar by John Mason is a perfect example of this: fully realized, clearly elucidated, crisp, precise, but with a turn or twist to the various components that endows the elegant form not only with motion, but with a tense energy that elicits a sense of apprehension or anxiety.

This feeling of uneasiness or disquietude is found under many guises in the arts today, a reflection of a world in crisis. It can be expressed by iconic means, as Arneson and Notkin do; by overtones of the surreal, as Jack Earl does; or by formal means, as in the work of Mason, Gustin, and Huntoon. In much of the work throughout this exhibition there is a semblance of conceit, of mannerism, but not in the pejorative sense of the terms. There are eccentricities, and tensions, but these have not gotten out of hand.

Perhaps the most telling aspect of the juried exhibition is the change in direction signified by the appearance of a certain formalism and refinement in much of the work. These pieces are well-crafted and exhibit a concern with perfection, or precision, like much of contemporary Japanese work. An elegance and refinement has reappeared, and there is a careful concern for detail. Surfaces are smooth, often polished. Color is subtle (though sometimes bright), often deep and rich. Decoration is often exquisitely detailed. Sometimes the bottoms and inner surfaces of lids are carefully glazed and decorated, as in the jar by Roseline Delisle. And like contemporary Japanese ceramics, there is a preciousness to many of these pieces. There is a tendency toward smaller, finely wrought objects with exquisite glaze effects, subtle textures, and wonderfully tactile surfaces. Ron Nagle's tiny *Black Knob Job,* with its subtle pink droplets and deep Persian-blue base (seen only when the piece can be handled) is stunning in its simplicity, yet lush and rich. One yearns to touch it.

Adrian Saxe's untitled jar, though larger than some of his previous work, is elegant and adventuresome; the deep jade-green of its glossy surface is a surprising contrast to the lavalike rock formation upon which it sits. Nancy Adams combines careful detailing and unusual coloration in her *Spirit Corn Vessel.* Jim Caswell and Itsue Ito both produce opulent works with brilliant color and highly glazed surfaces, while Tom Rippon combines subtle tones of beige and gray applied with great precision to achieve a wonderfully sophisticated porcelain form. These pieces are simply a pleasure to behold; we are enchanted. Mrs. Robineau, indeed, would be pleased.

This preciousness and opulence have been accompanied, of necessity, by a revival of interest in technique. During the past two decades, artists have concentrated on the material itself, using it to express its own qualities. Just as expressionist paintings were about the qualities of paint as much as anything else, expressionist ceramics explored the properties of clay. These works told of the malleability of clay, describing its texture and manipulative possibilities. Unglazed surfaces left the basic material exposed. But this new sensibility demands a different kind of technique, one of controlled glazing, of detailed modeling, and careful finishing. There is no room for the unexpected, or any miscalculation. A reliance on accident has been replaced by a knowledgeability of materials that verges on virtuosity, giving the artist the control needed to create such precious, urbane objects.

It remains to be seen whether these new works do signal a change in the deeper currents of contemporary clay art or whether these characteristics are only an eddy, soon to be swept along by another wash. This should be clear by the time of the next *Ceramic National.*

BARBARA PERRY, PhD
Curator of Ceramics, Everson Museum of Art

INVITATIONAL

ROBERT ARNESON
Clay I Am, It Is True,
1982-83
stoneware
83 x 25 x 25

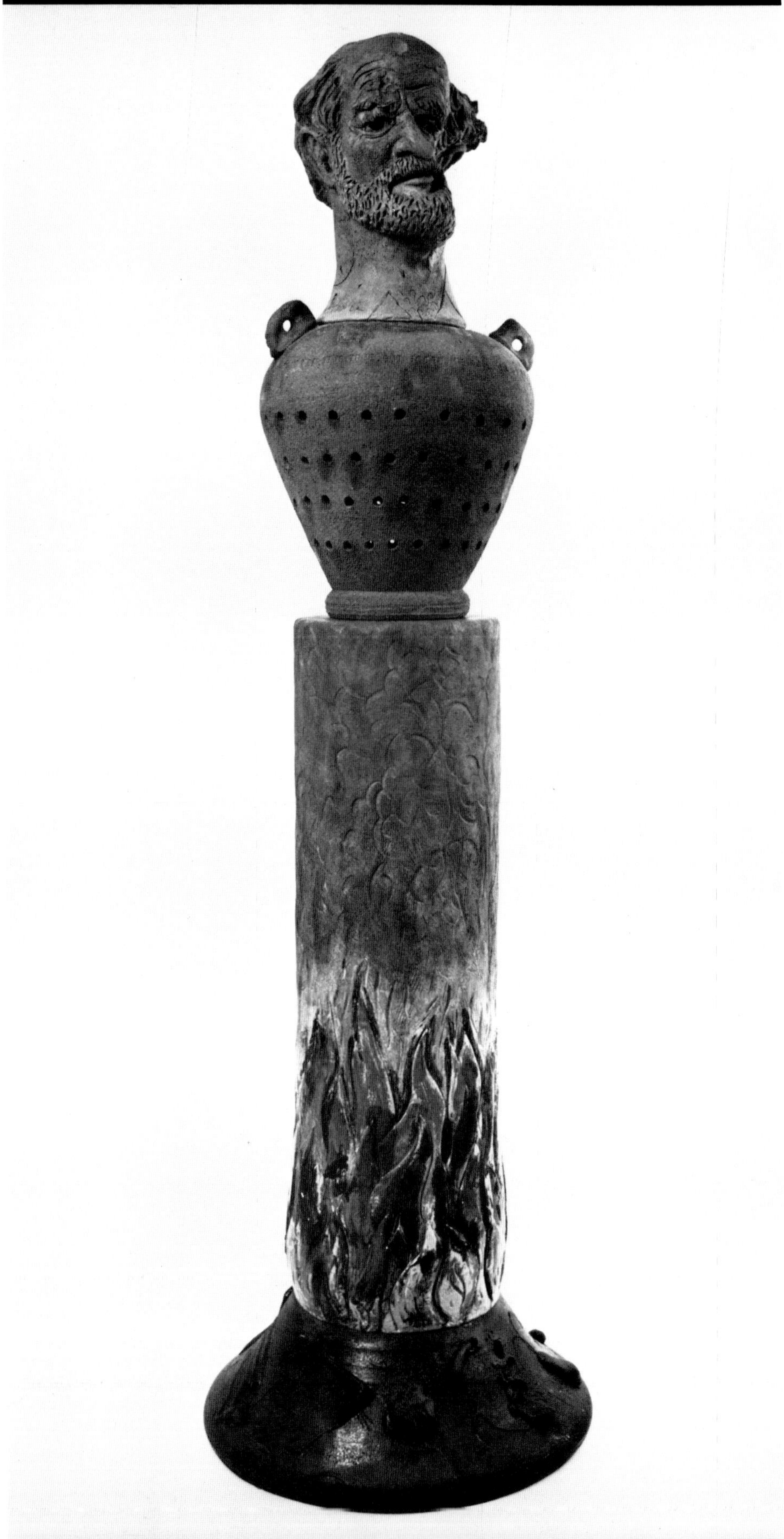

RUDY AUTIO
Goodbye to the Girls on Galena Street,
1986
stoneware
36 x 26 x 25

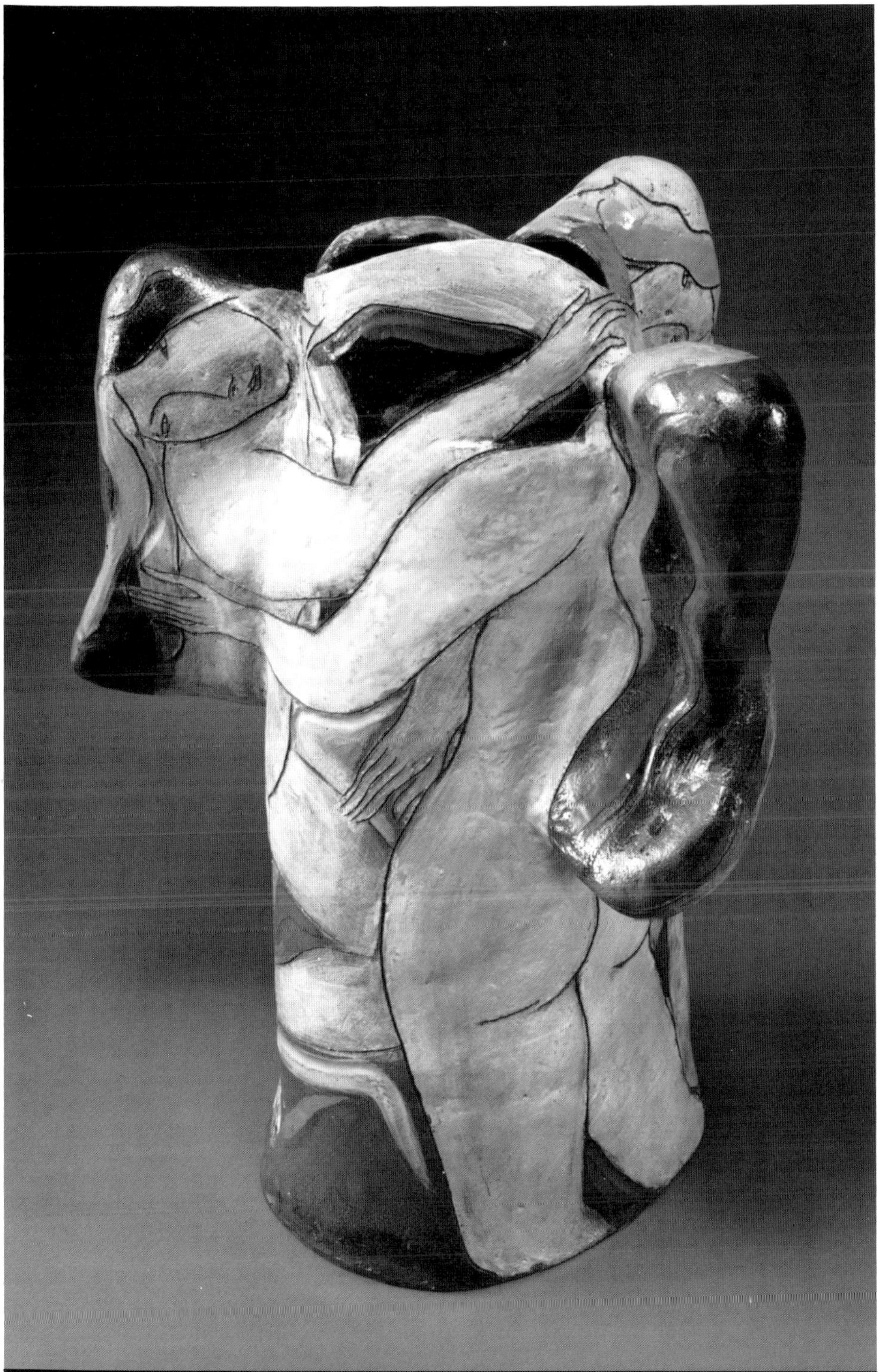

WILLIAM DALEY
Oval Chamber, 1986
stoneware
39½ x 18 x 23

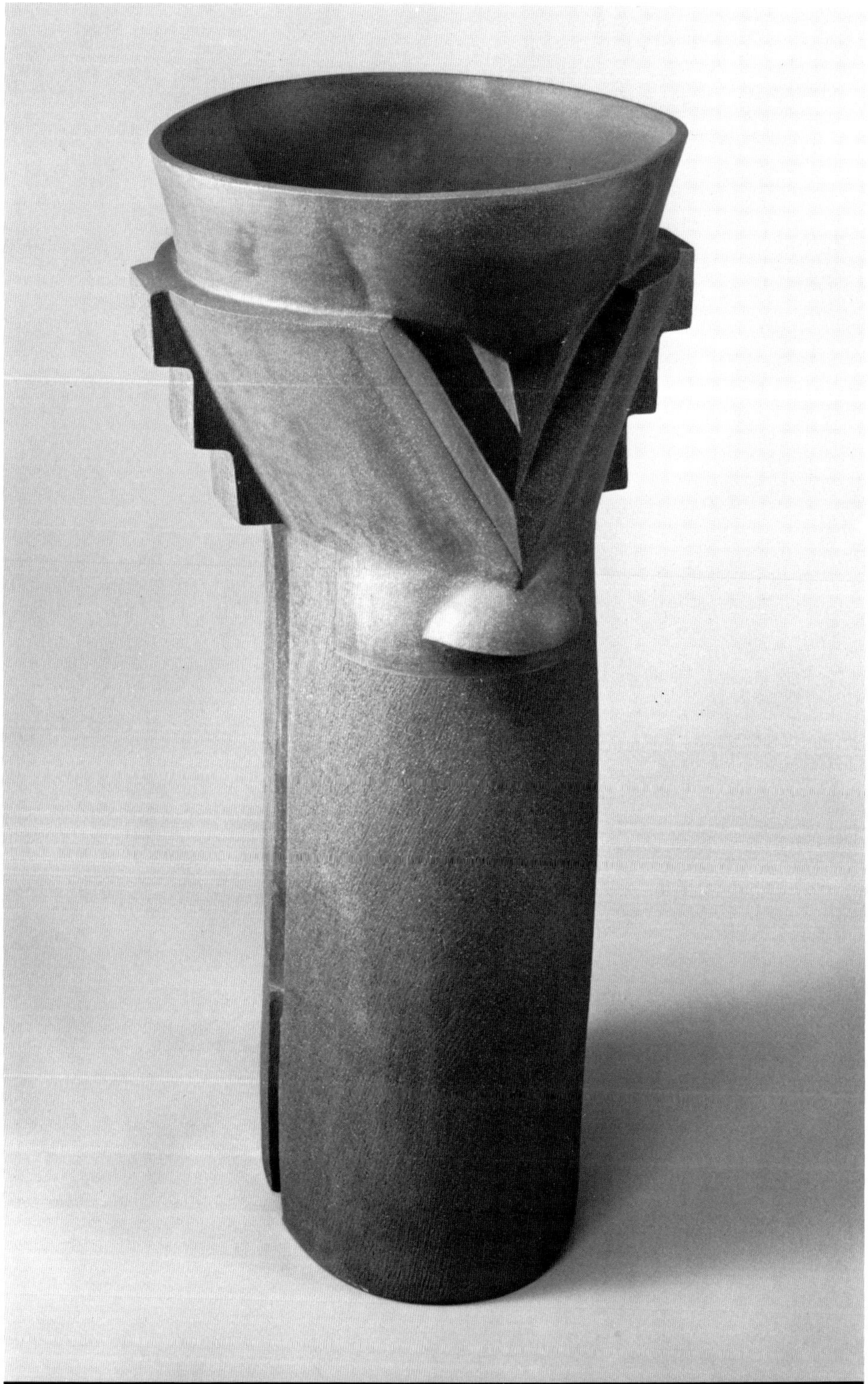

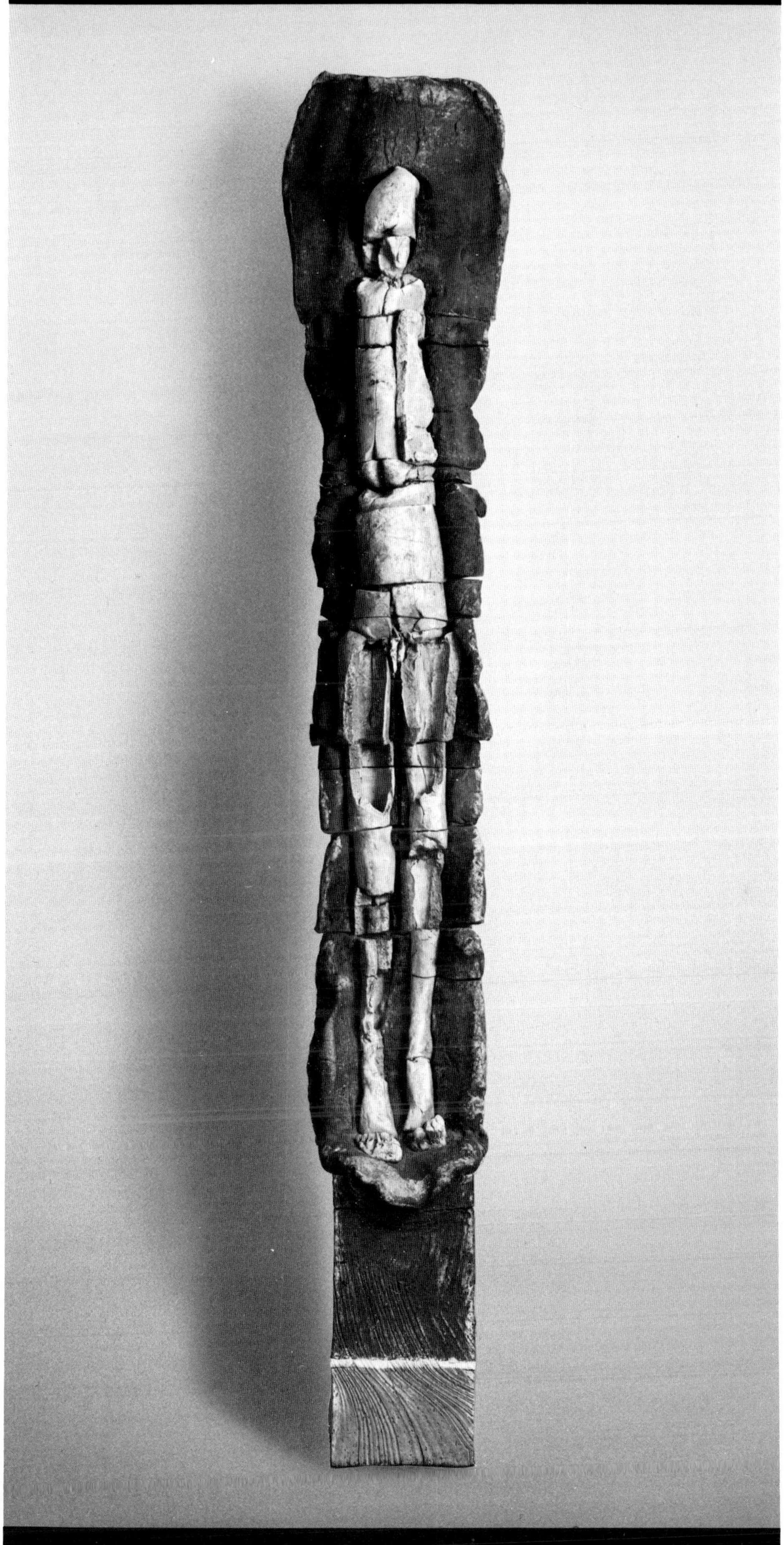

STEPHEN DE STAEBLER
Standing Figure with Dark Aura, 1984
stoneware
99 x 18 x 21

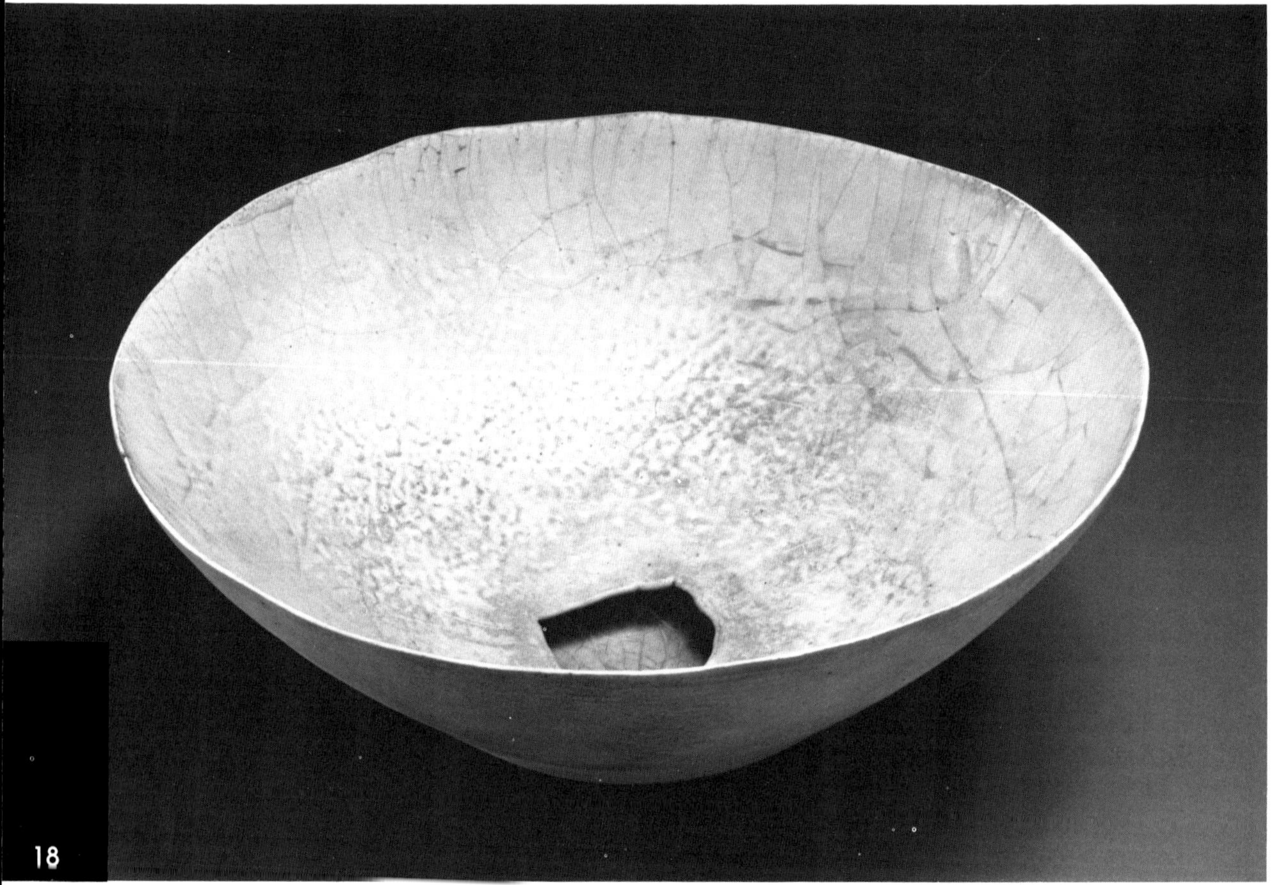

RICHARD DE VORE
Pot #363, 1983
stoneware
6¾ x 15½ diam.

JACK EARL
He Looked and Found NOMAN, 1986
earthenware
28½ x 19 x 22¼

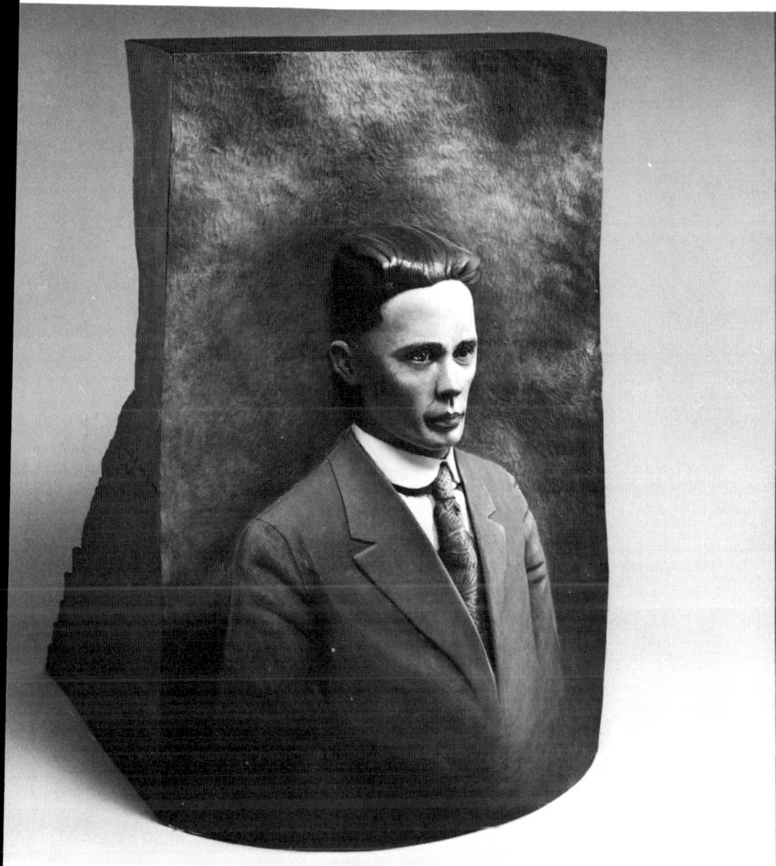

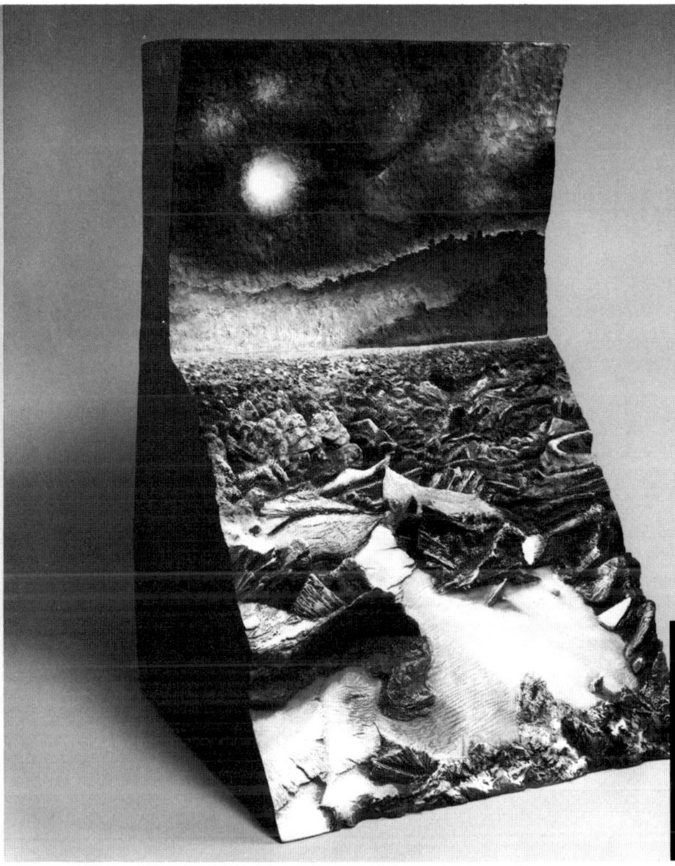

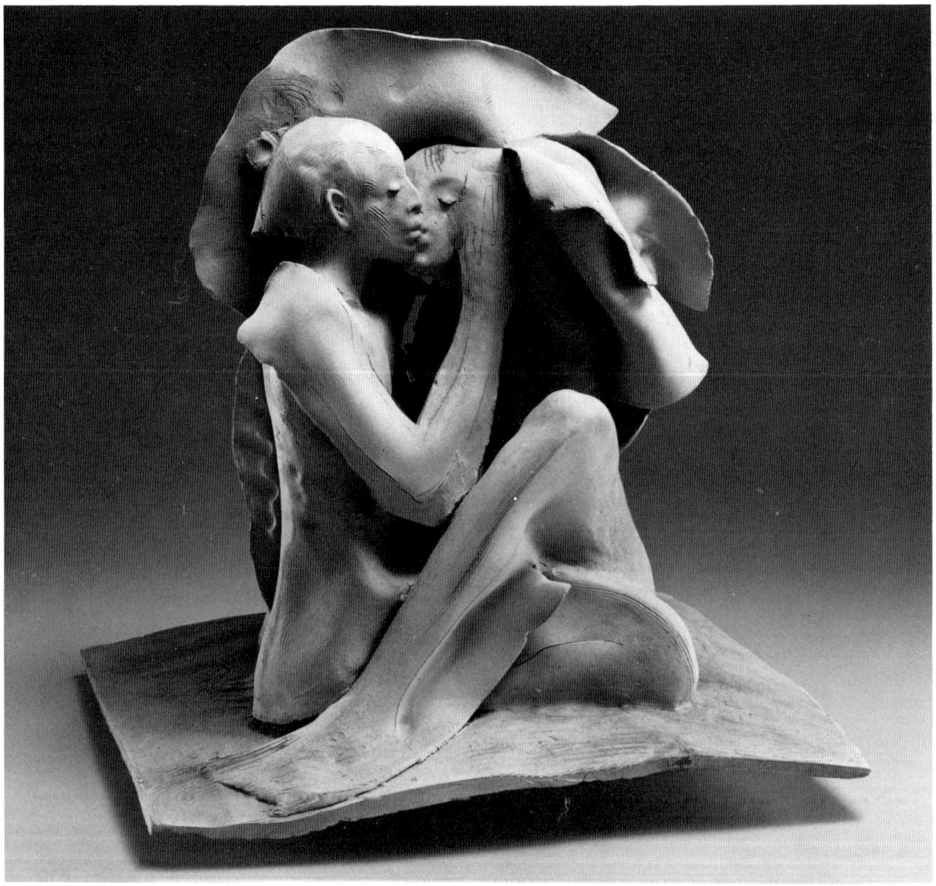

MARY FRANK
Lovers, 1983
earthenware
21½ x 21½ x 15

VIOLA FREY
Untitled (Man/Nude/Woman/Figurines), 1986
earthenware
39½ x 19½ x 16

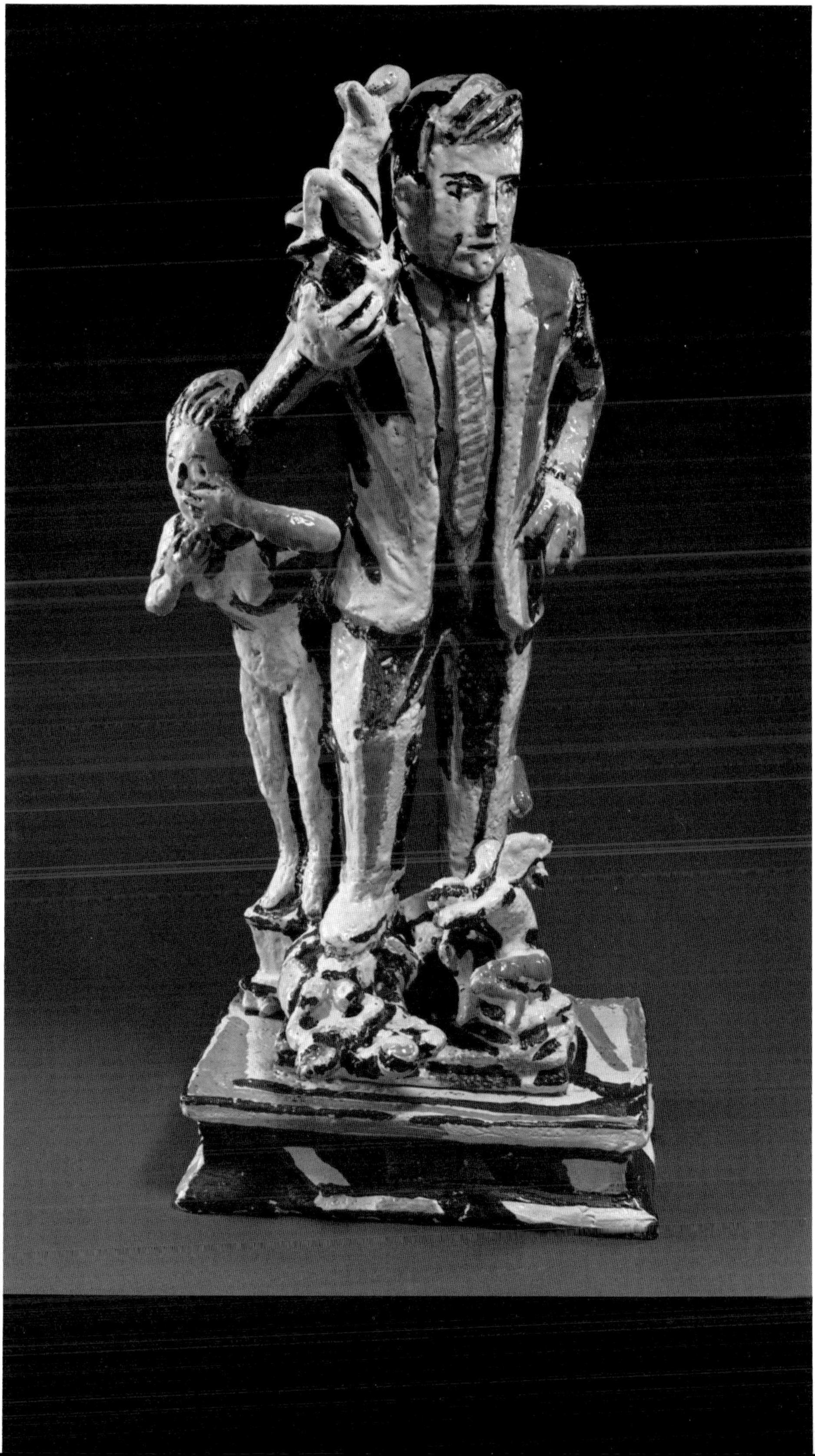

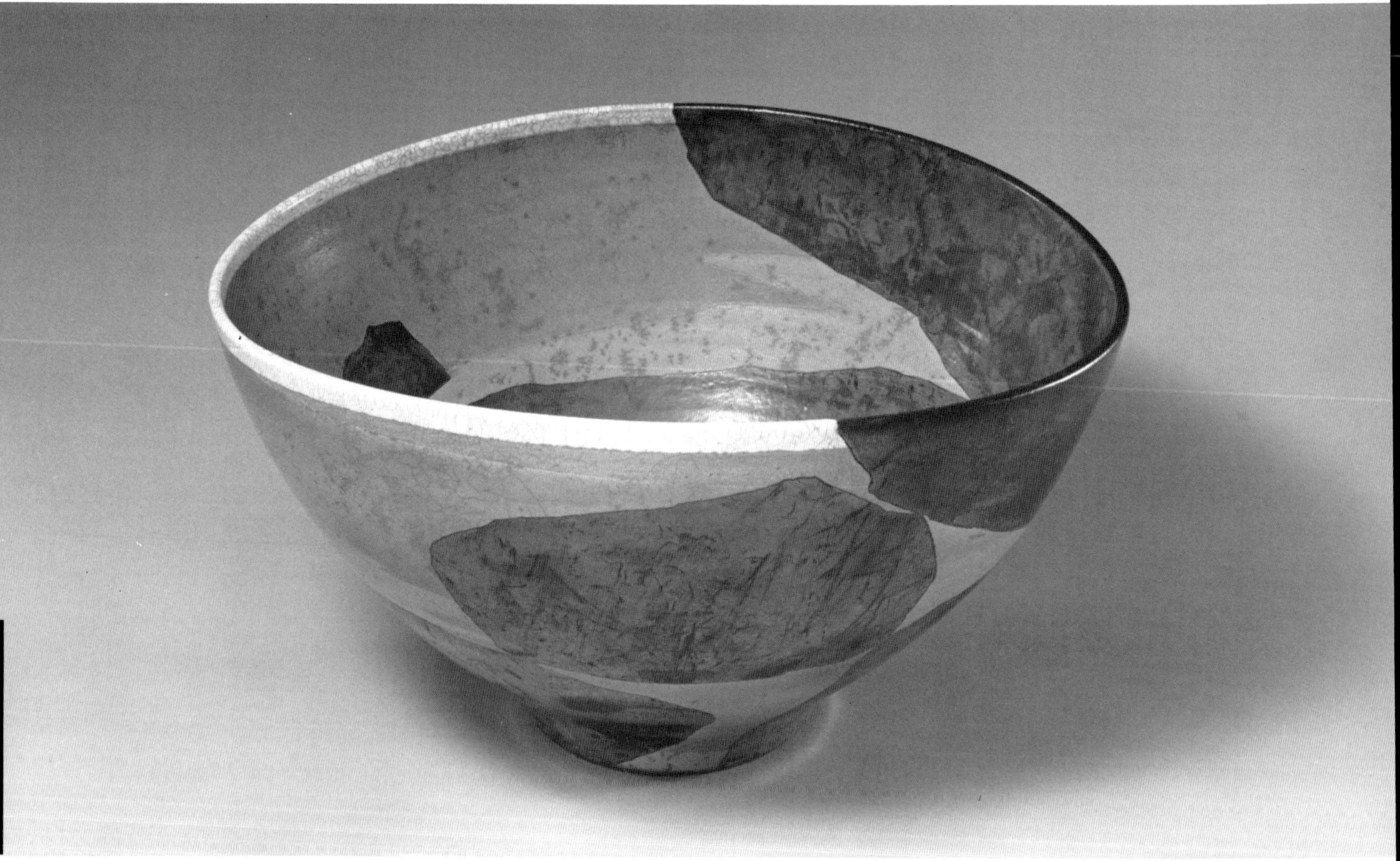

WAYNE HIGBY
Mammoth Rock Beach, 1984
earthenware
10½ x 19 x 16

JUN KANEKO
Untitled, 1986
stoneware
32 x 17 x 20

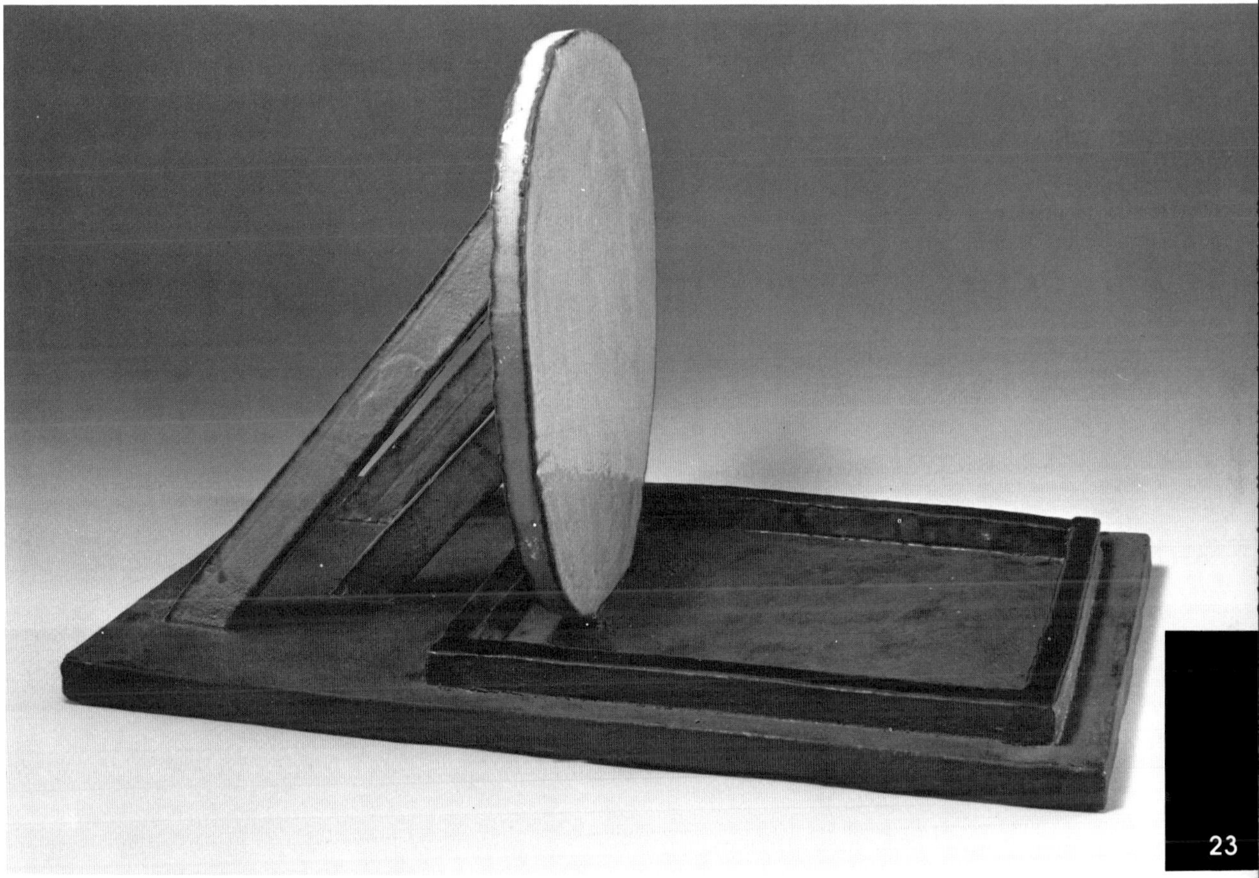

JOHN MASON
Untitled, 1984
stoneware
16 x 13 x 13

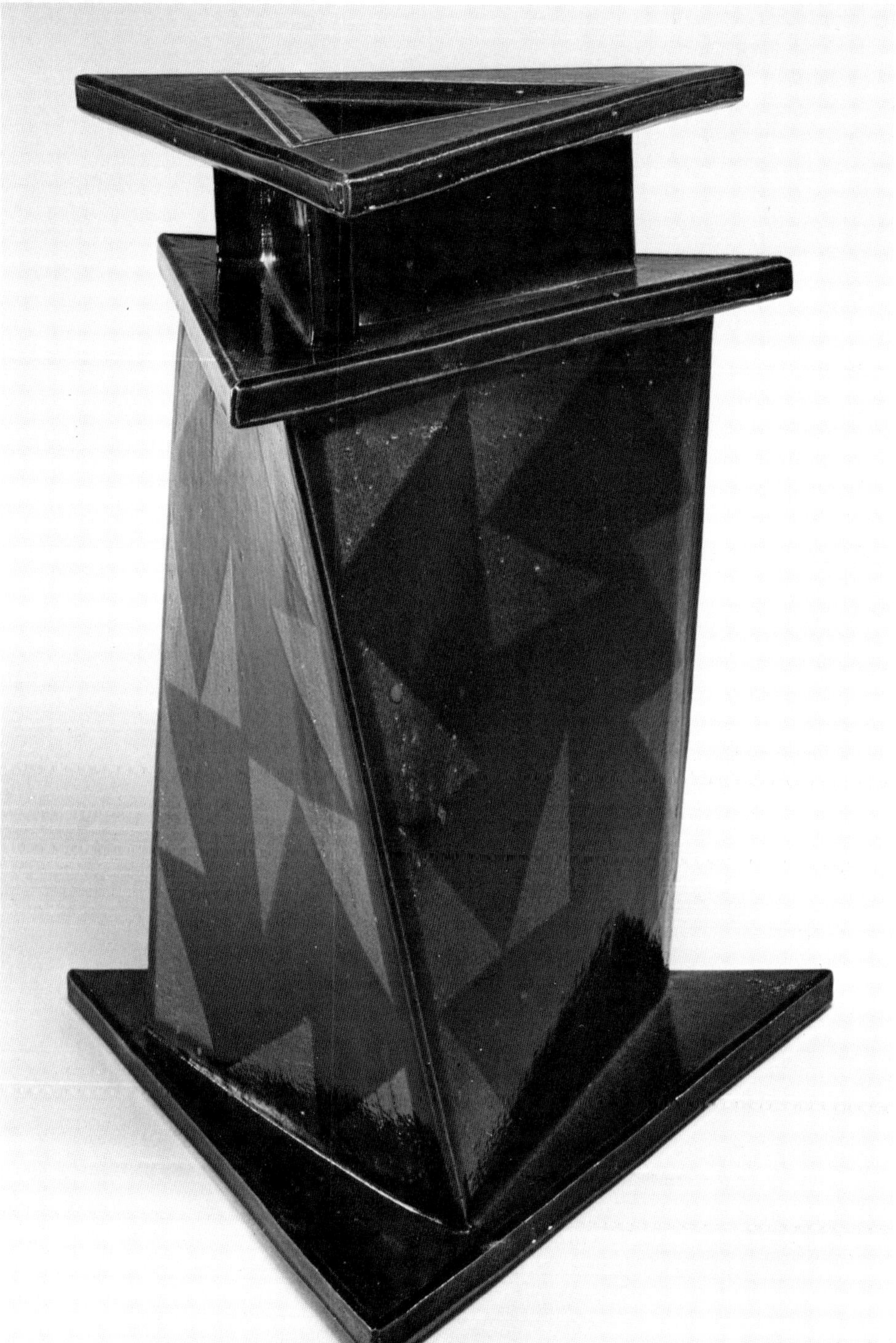

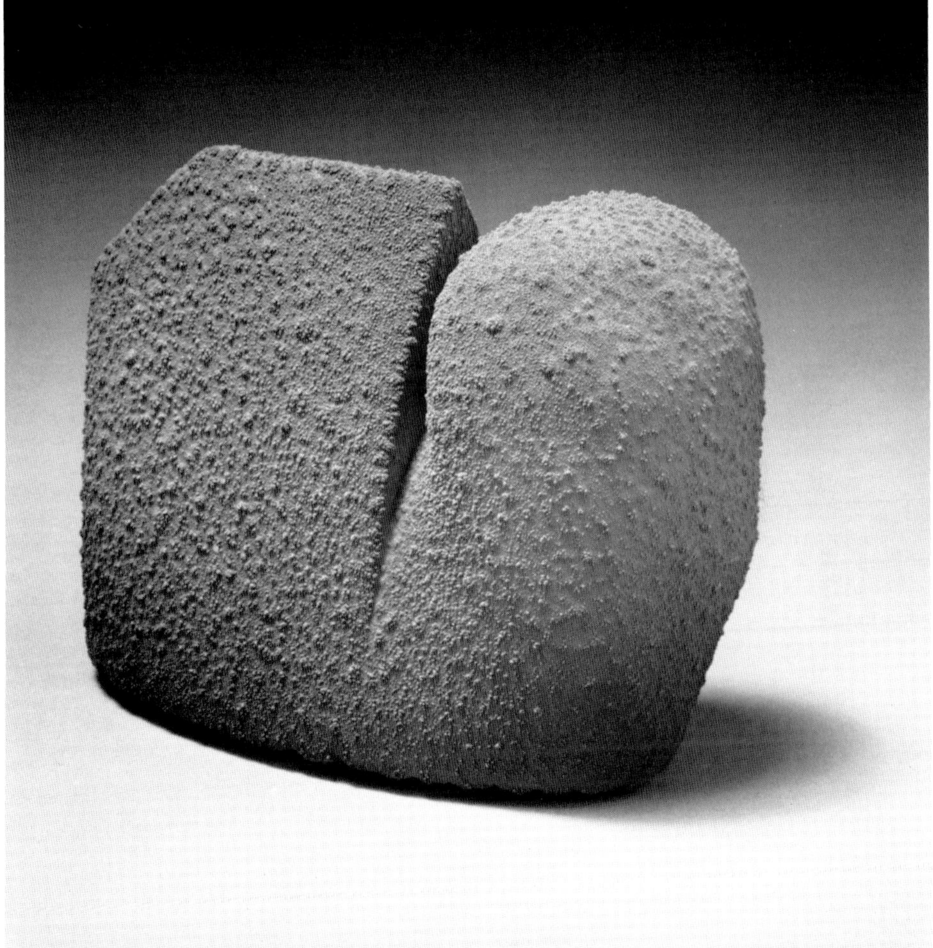

RON NAGLE
Orange Tracy, 1986
earthenware
3¼ x 4 x 1¾

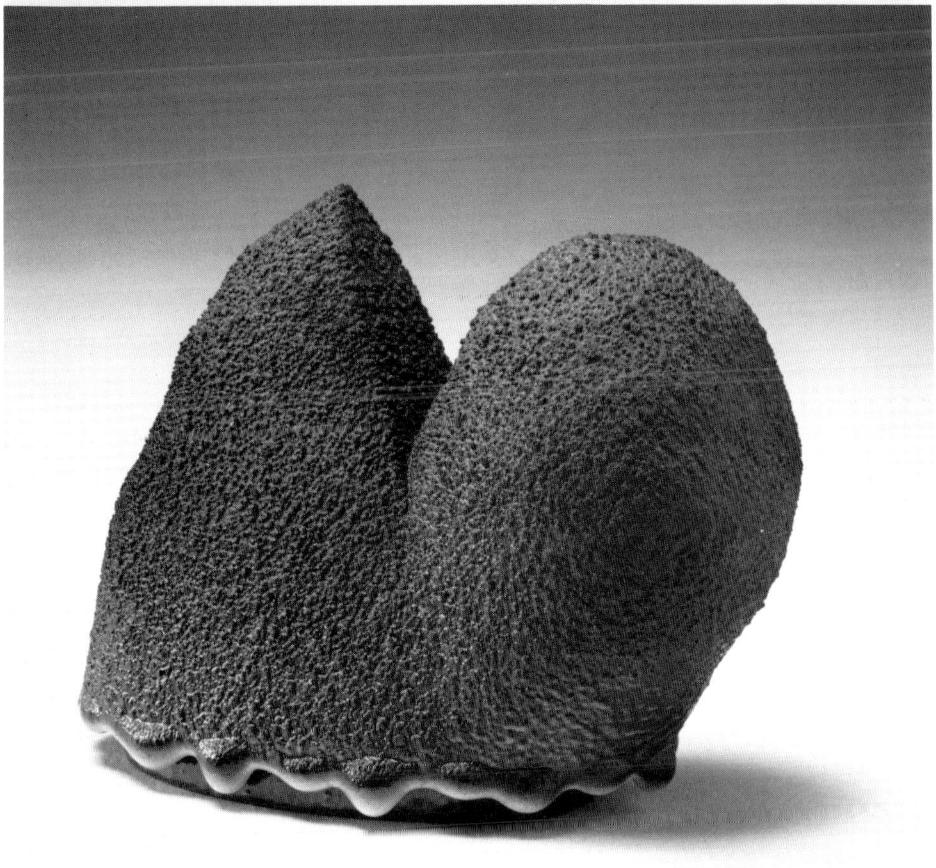

RON NAGLE
Black Knob Job, 1984
earthenware
3¼ x 4 x 1¾

KEN PRICE
Club Atomica, 1986
earthenware
15 x 9½ diam.

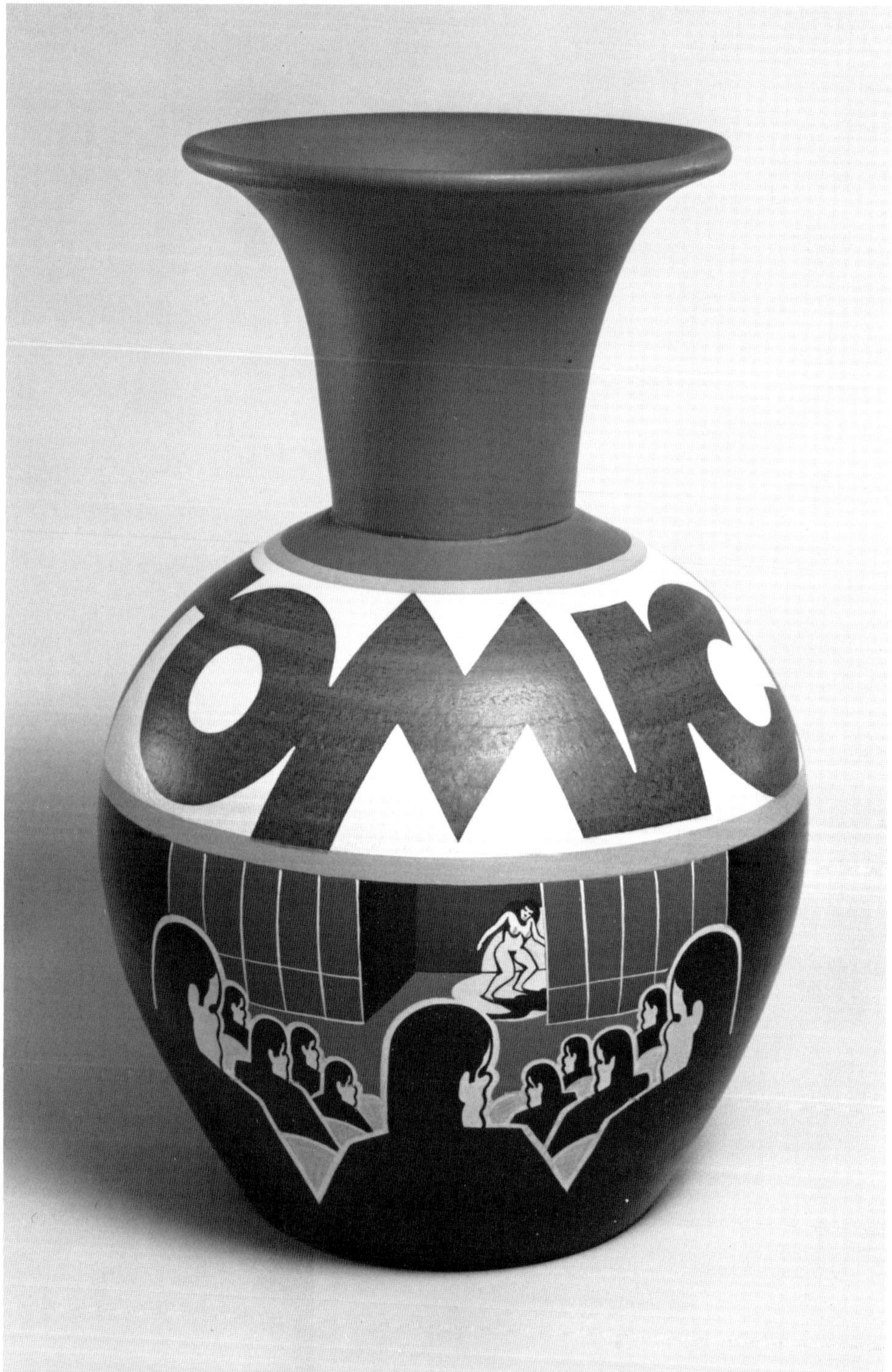

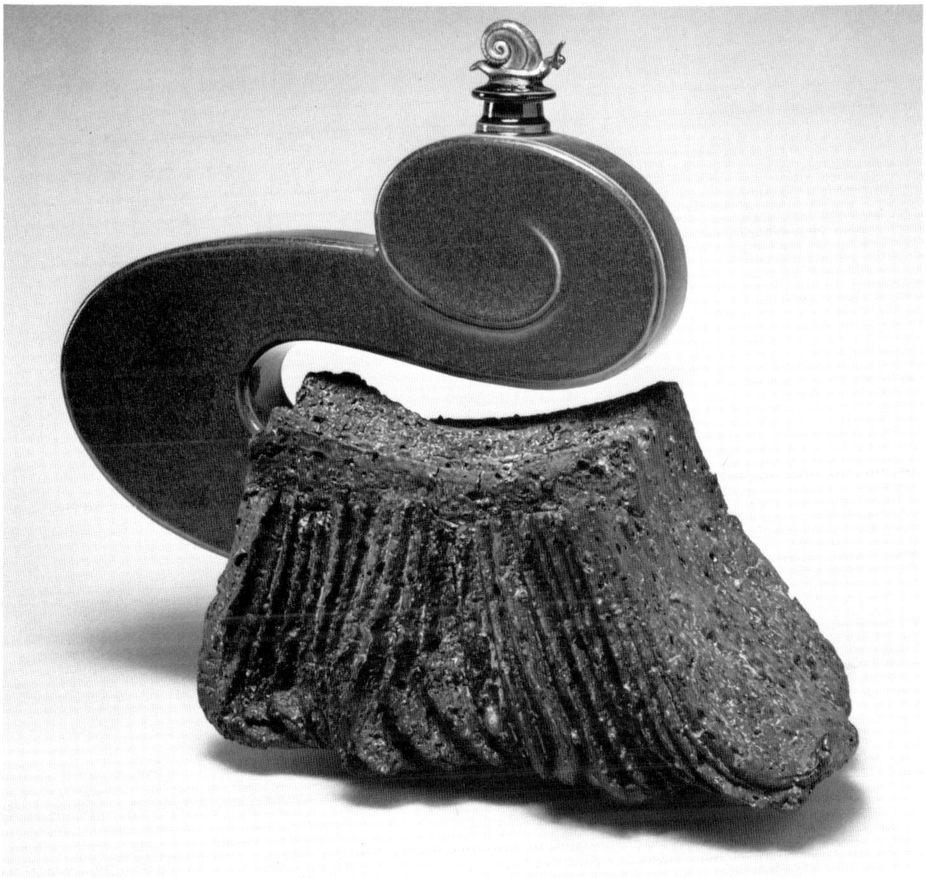

ADRIAN SAXE
Untitled Jar, 1985
porcelain and stoneware
13 x 9½ x 15½

RICHARD SHAW
Paper Lighthouse, 1985
porcelain
21 x 20 x 9

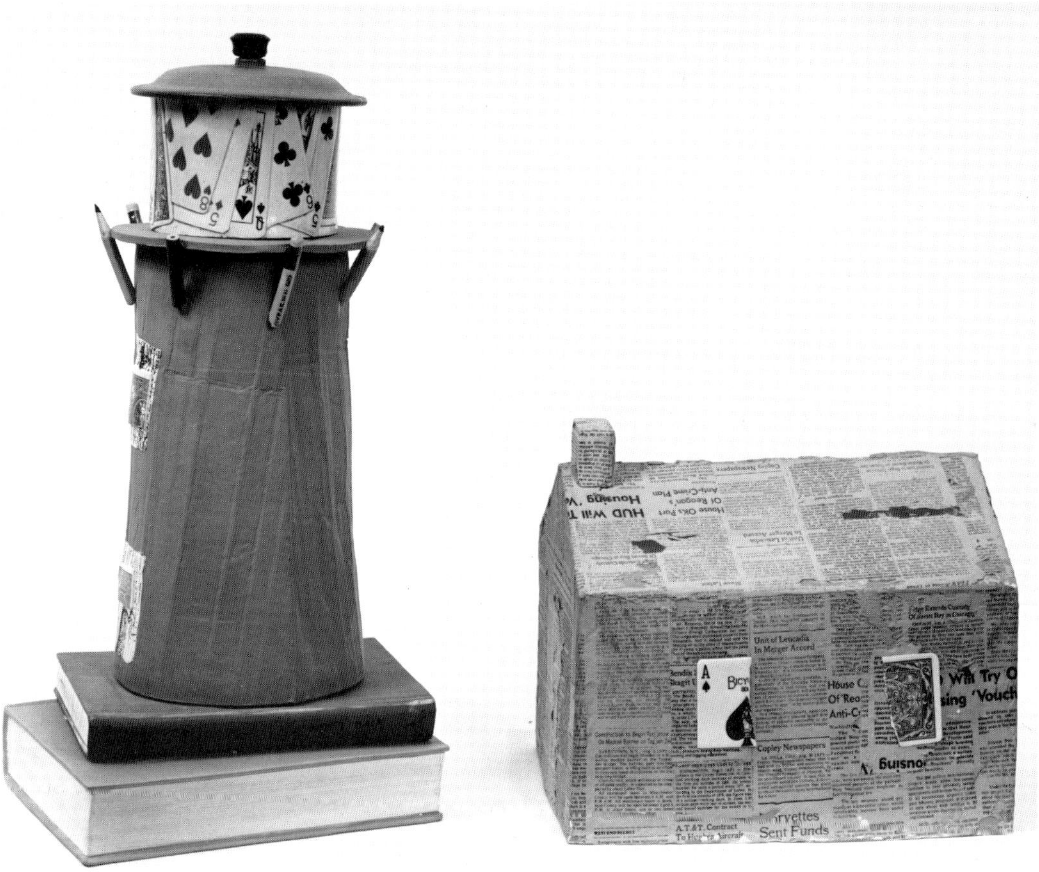

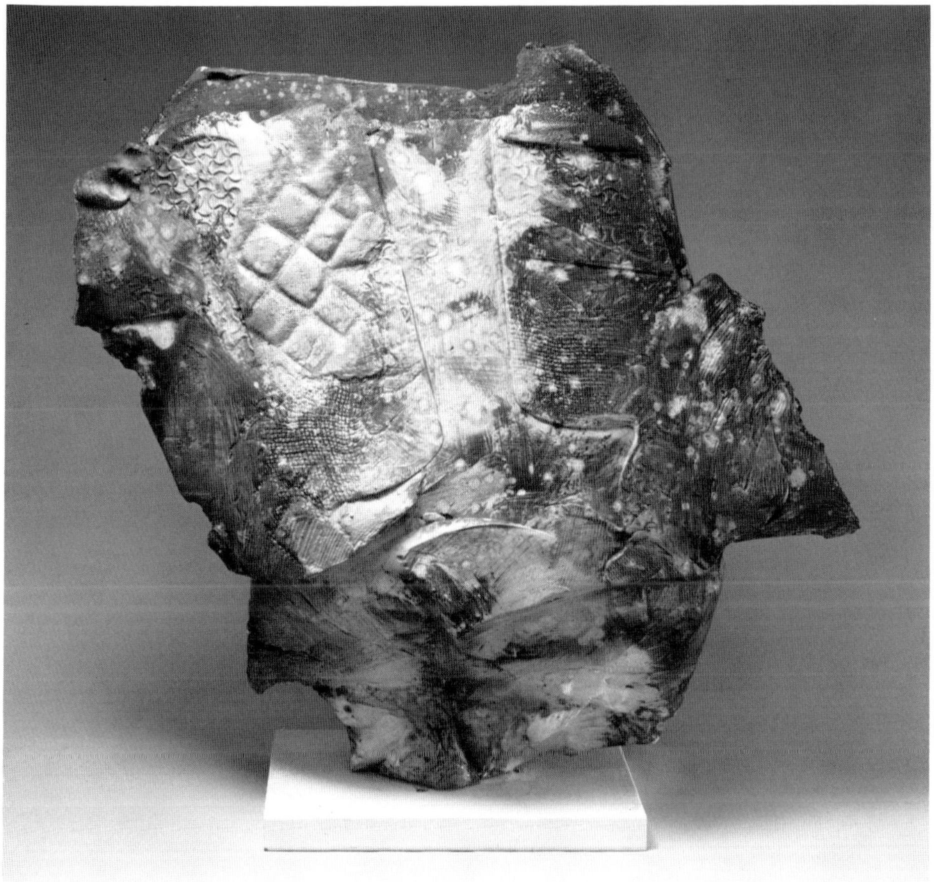

PAUL SOLDNER
Pedestal Piece, 1985
earthenware
30 x 32 x 7

RUDOLF STAFFEL
Untitled, 1986
porcelain
7½ x 4½ x 4½

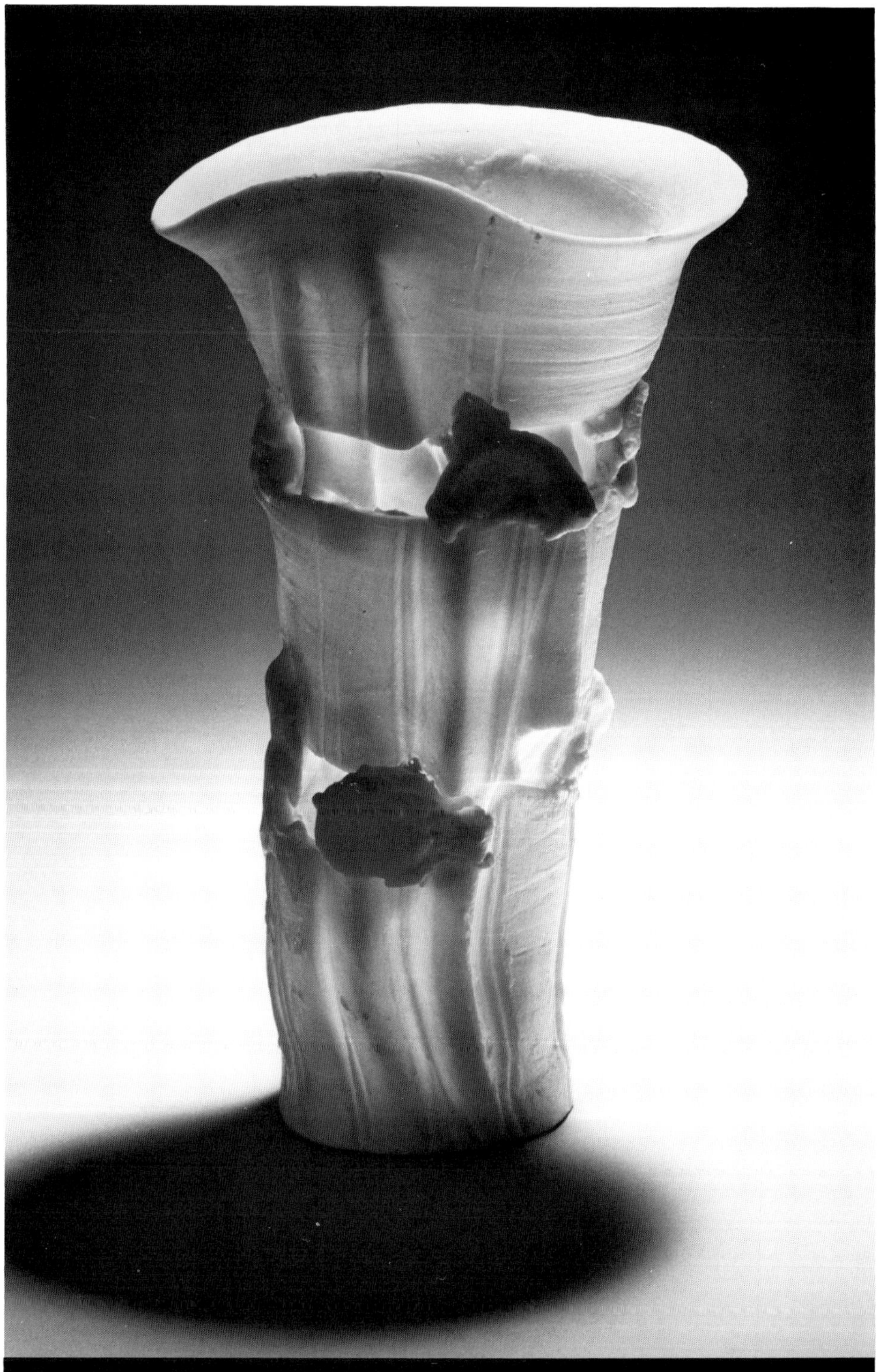

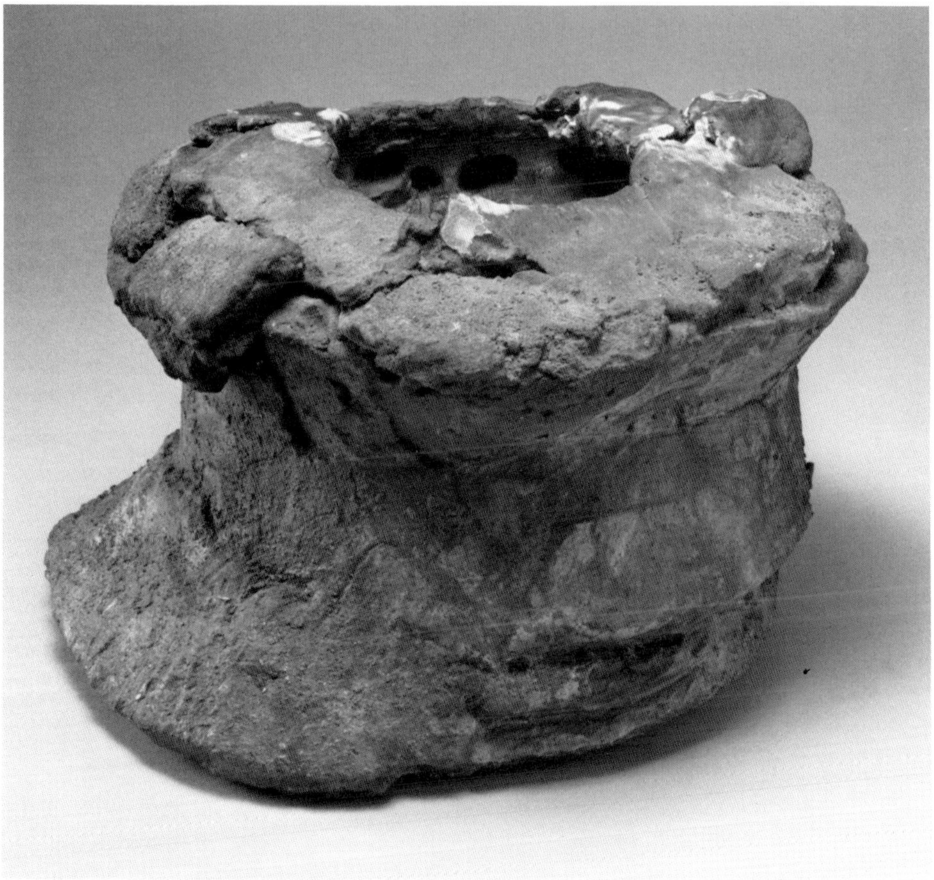

PETER VOULKOS
Untitled, 1983
earthenware
10½ x 13½ x 10

BETTY WOODMAN
Zante, 1985
earthenware
31 x 21 x 9

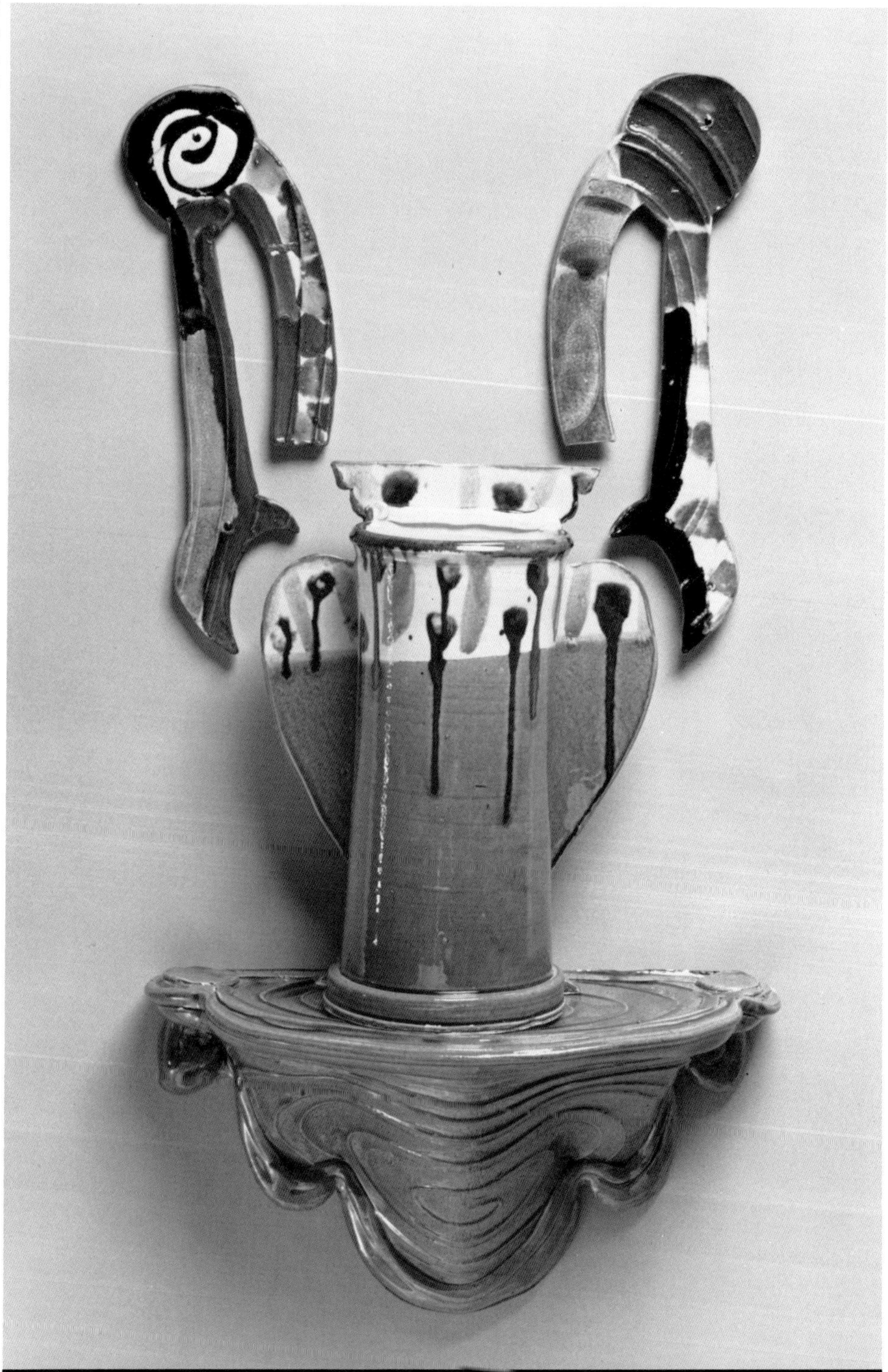

MARK BURNS, Vice Squad
Purchase prize with funds from the Dorothy and Robert Riester Ceramic Fund

BELINDA GABRYL, Tornado Teapot and Creamer
Purchase prize with funds from the Dorothy and Robert Riester Ceramic Fund

CLIFF GARTEN, Hatch, Hatch
Purchase prize with funds from the Dorothy and Robert Riester Ceramic Fund

CHRIS GUSTON, Vase
Purchase prize given by The Hancock Foundation

ITSUE ITO, Shutoh
Purchase prize given by The Hancock Foundation

JUDY MOONELIS, Curving Head
Purchase prize with funds from the Dorothy and Robert Riester Ceramic Fund

RICHARD NOTKIN, Cube Skull Teapot (Variation #6), Yixing Series
Purchase prize given by The Hancock Foundation

MARK BURNS
Vice Squad, 1985
earthenware, wood,
wire, paint
40 x 22 x 36

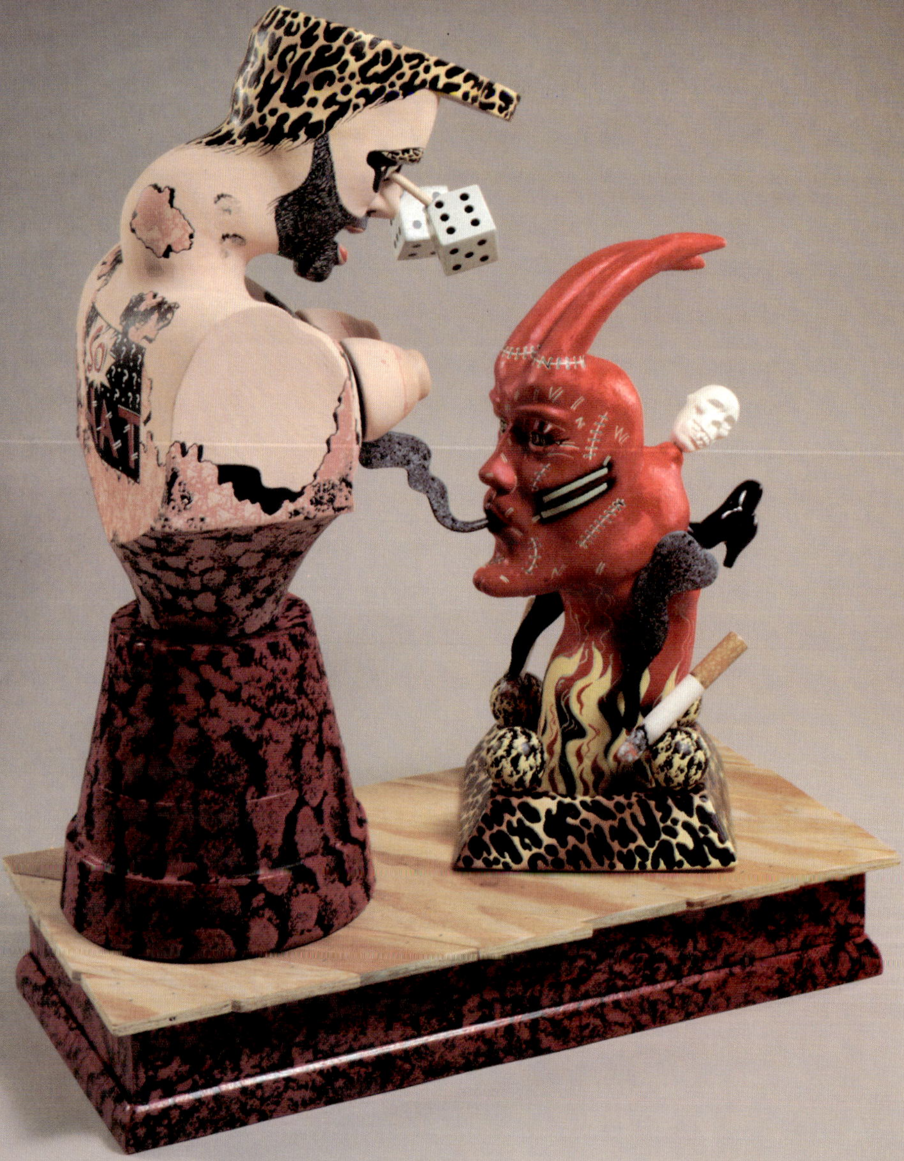

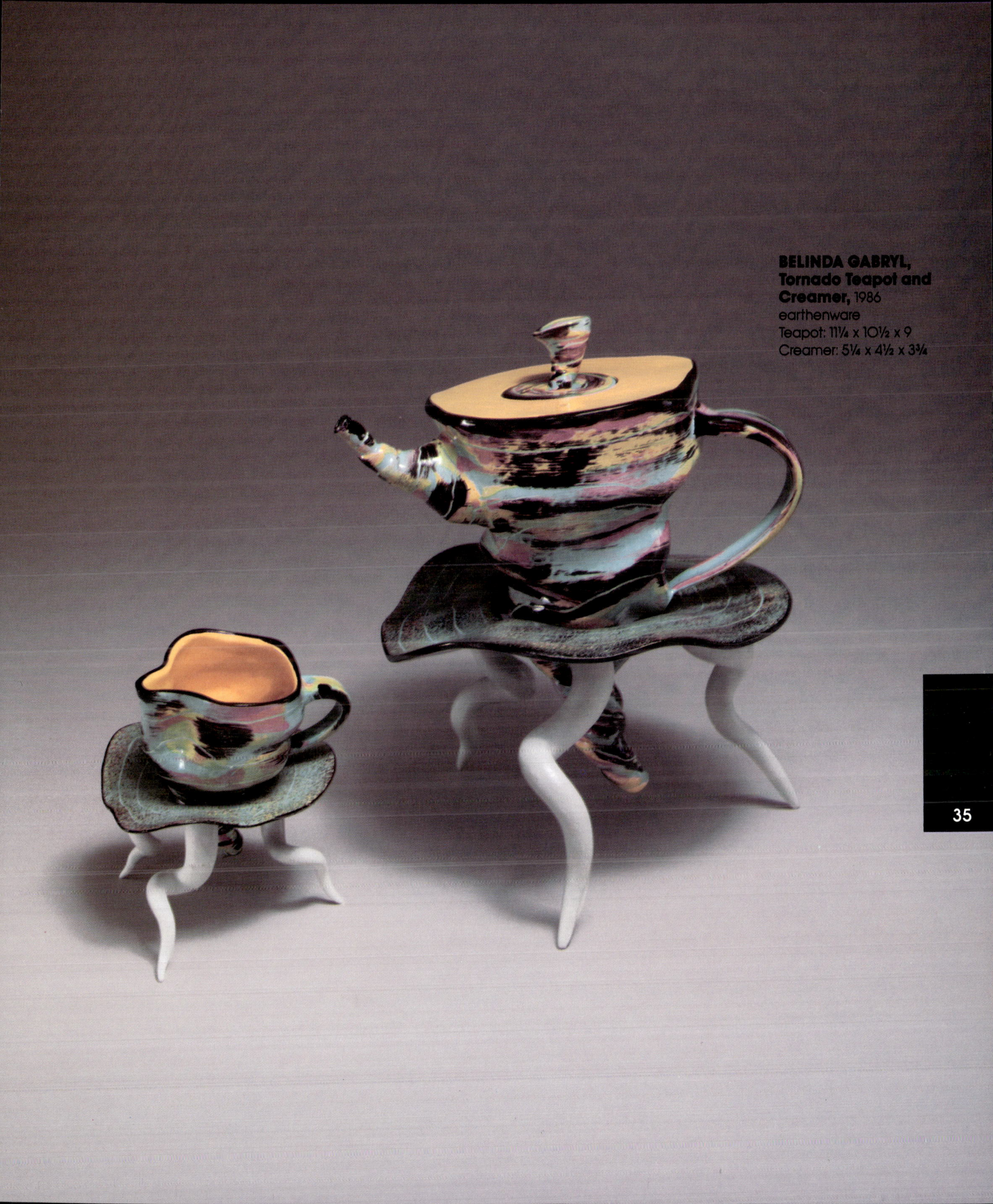

BELINDA GABRYL,
Tornado Teapot and Creamer, 1986
earthenware
Teapot: 11¼ x 10½ x 9
Creamer: 5¼ x 4½ x 3¾

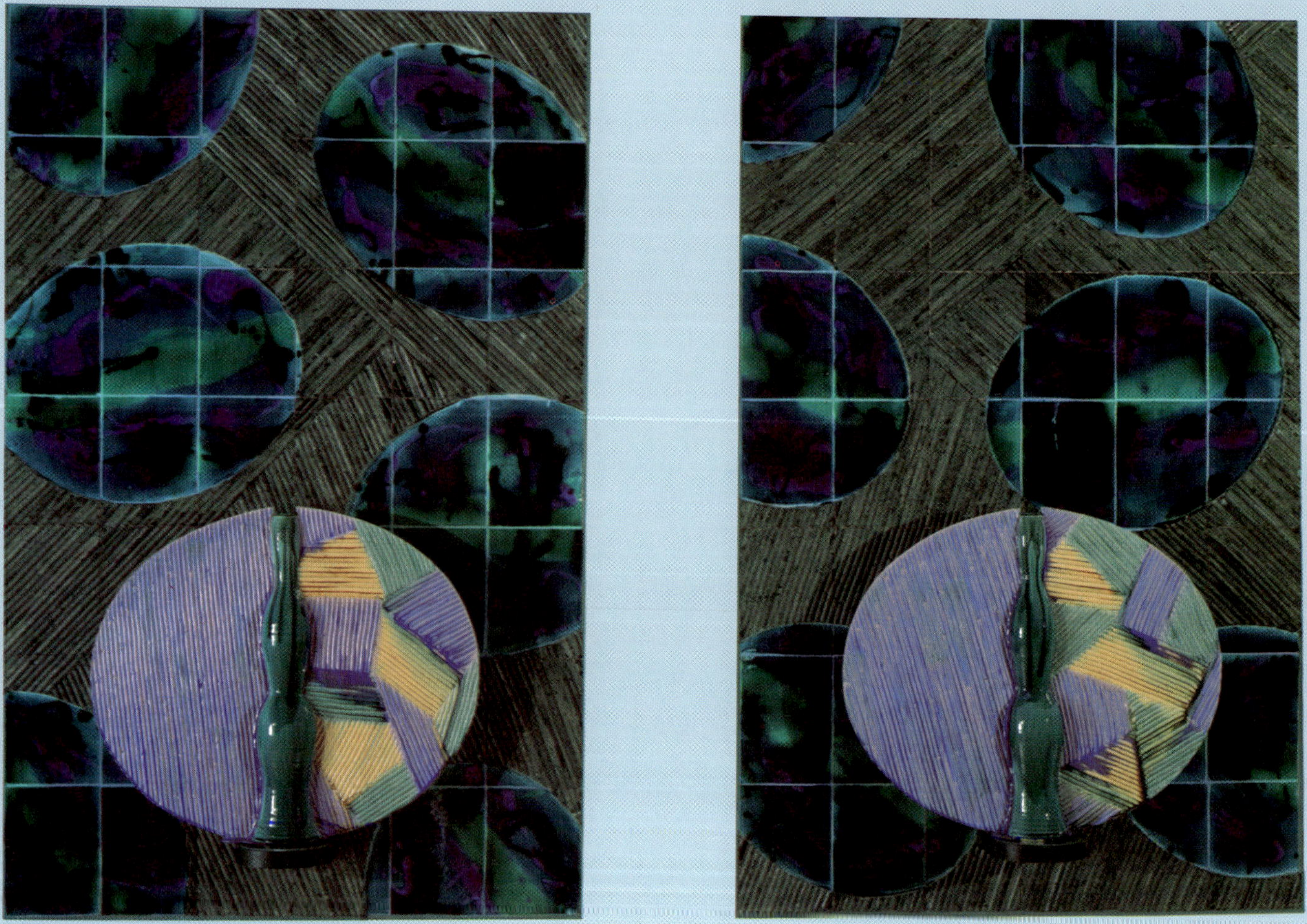

CLIFF GARTEN
Hatch, Hatch, 1984
earthenware
67½ x 41½ x 10¼

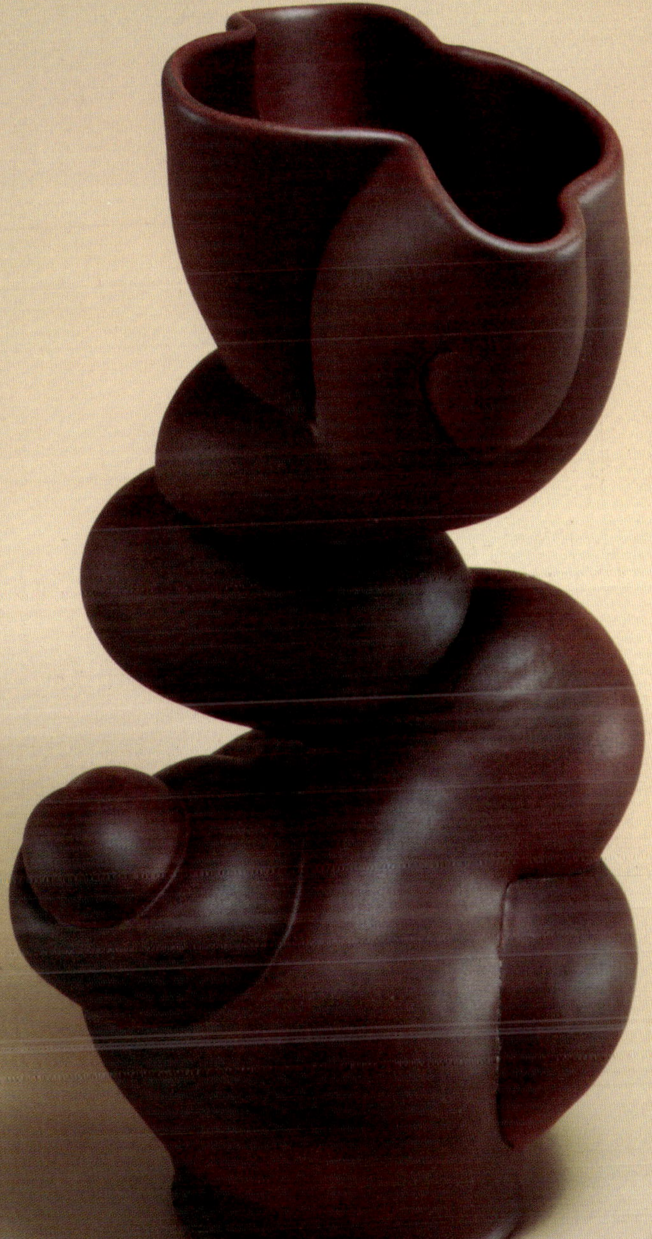

CHRIS GUSTIN,
Vase, 1986
stoneware
21 x 11 x 10

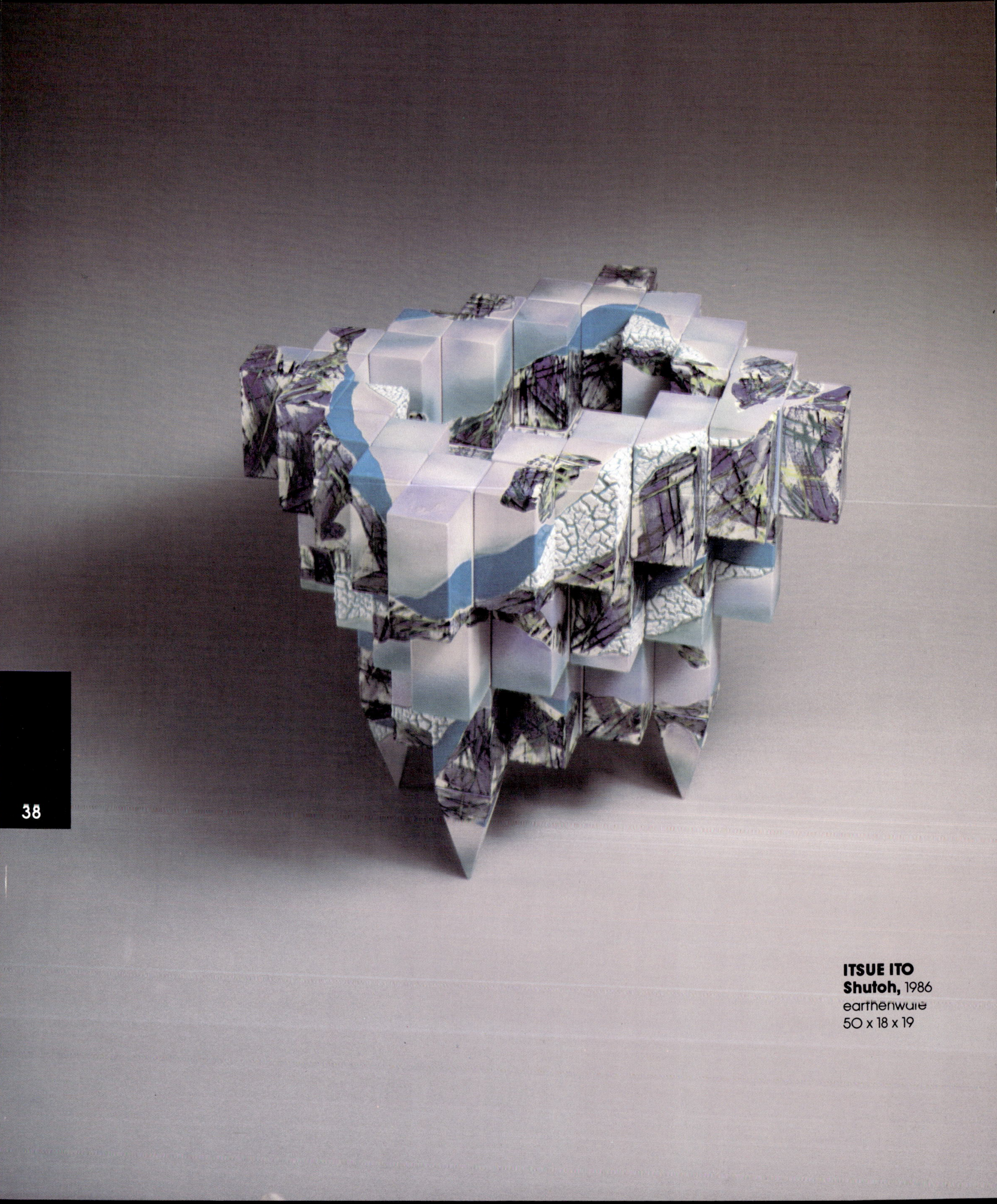

ITSUE ITO
Shutoh, 1986
earthenware
50 x 18 x 19

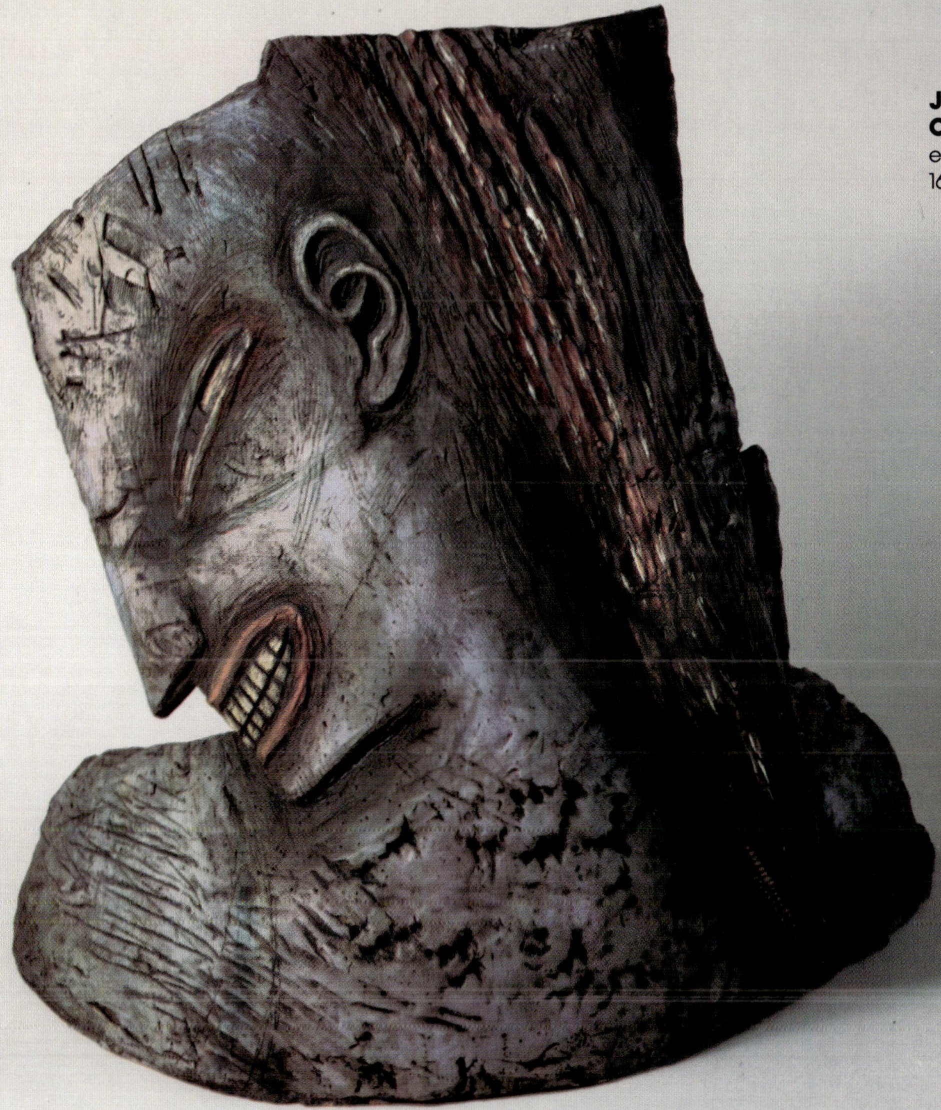

JUDY MOONELIS,
Curving Head, 1984-85
earthenware
16 x 27 x 13

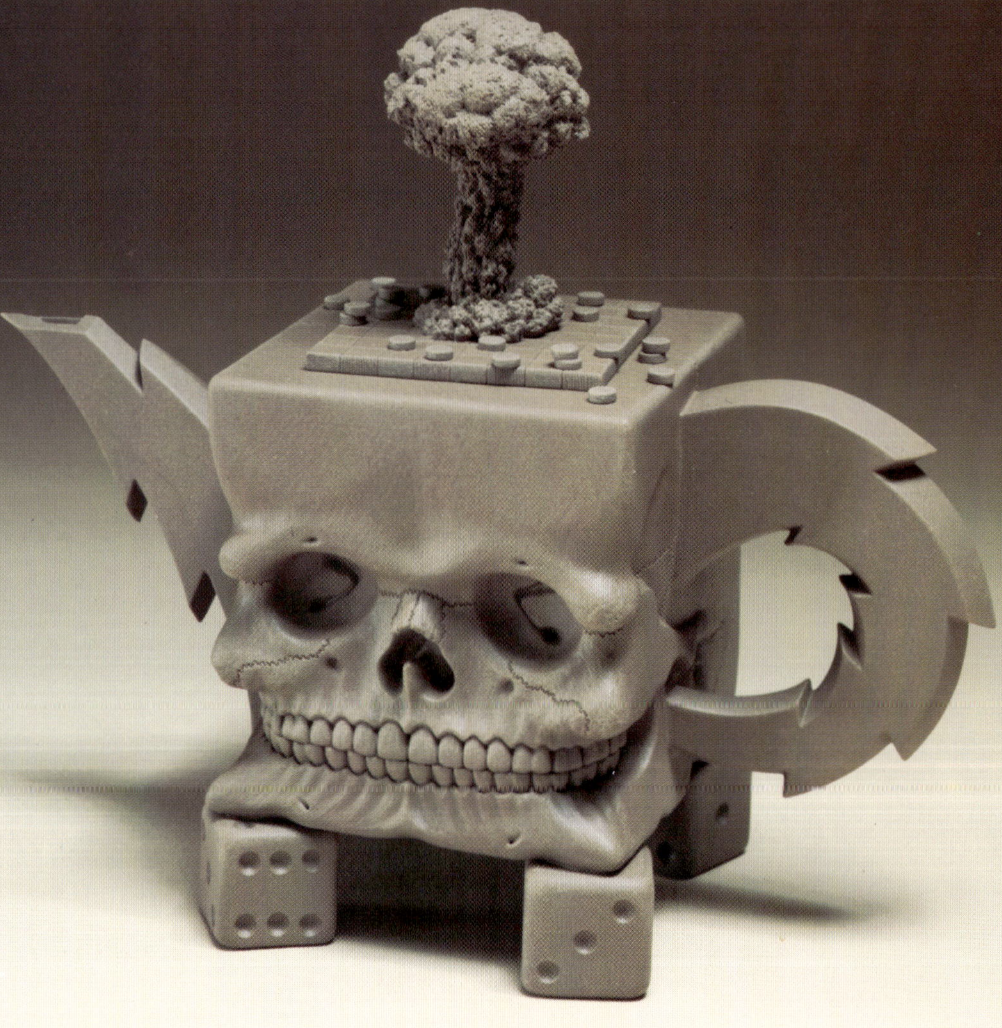

RICHARD NOTKIN,
***Cube Skull Teapot* (Variation #6),**
Yixing Series, 1985
stoneware
5¼ x 6 x 2¾

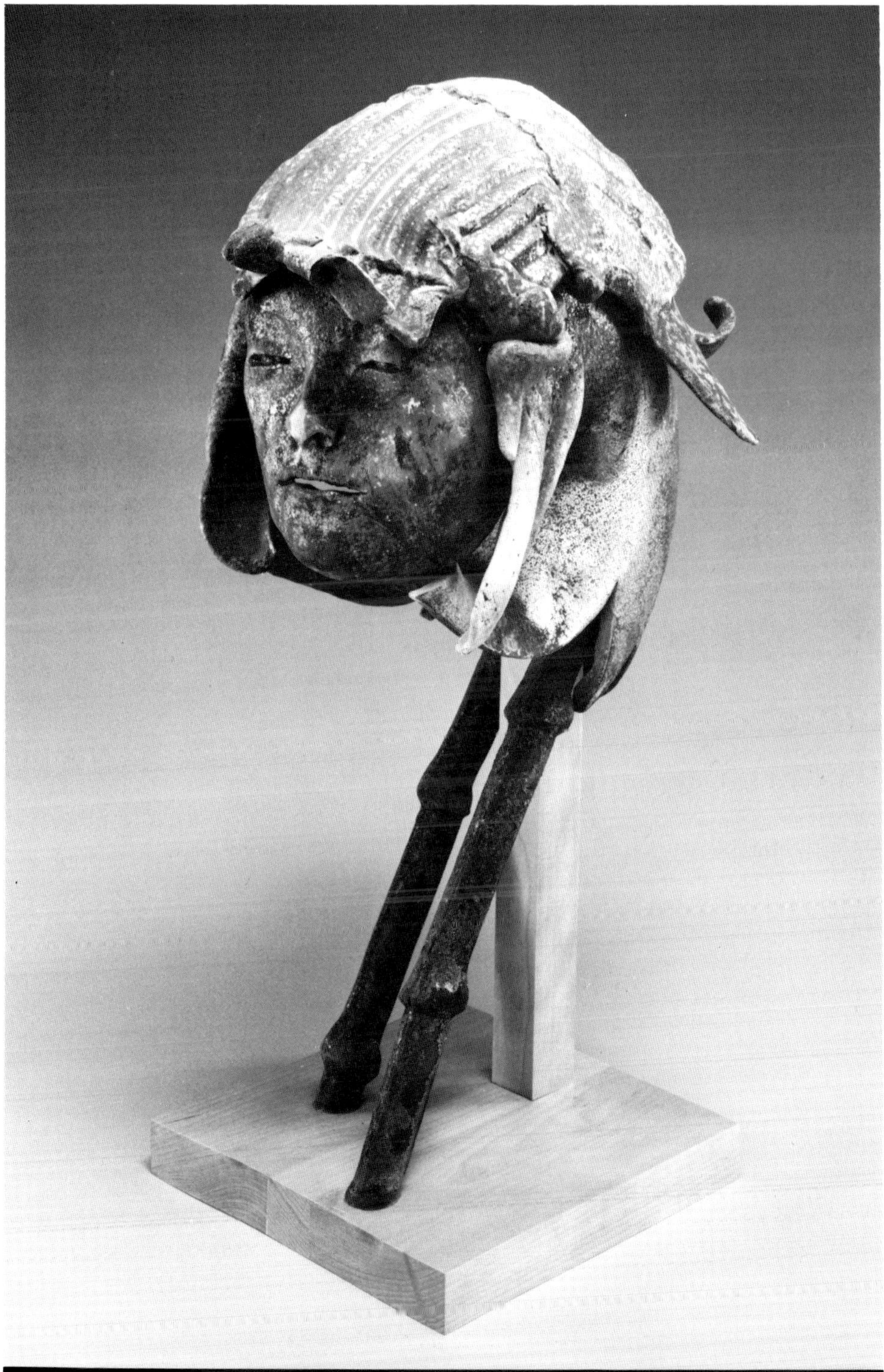

BILL ABRIGHT
Rice Lady, 1986
stoneware, wood
22 x 10 x 13

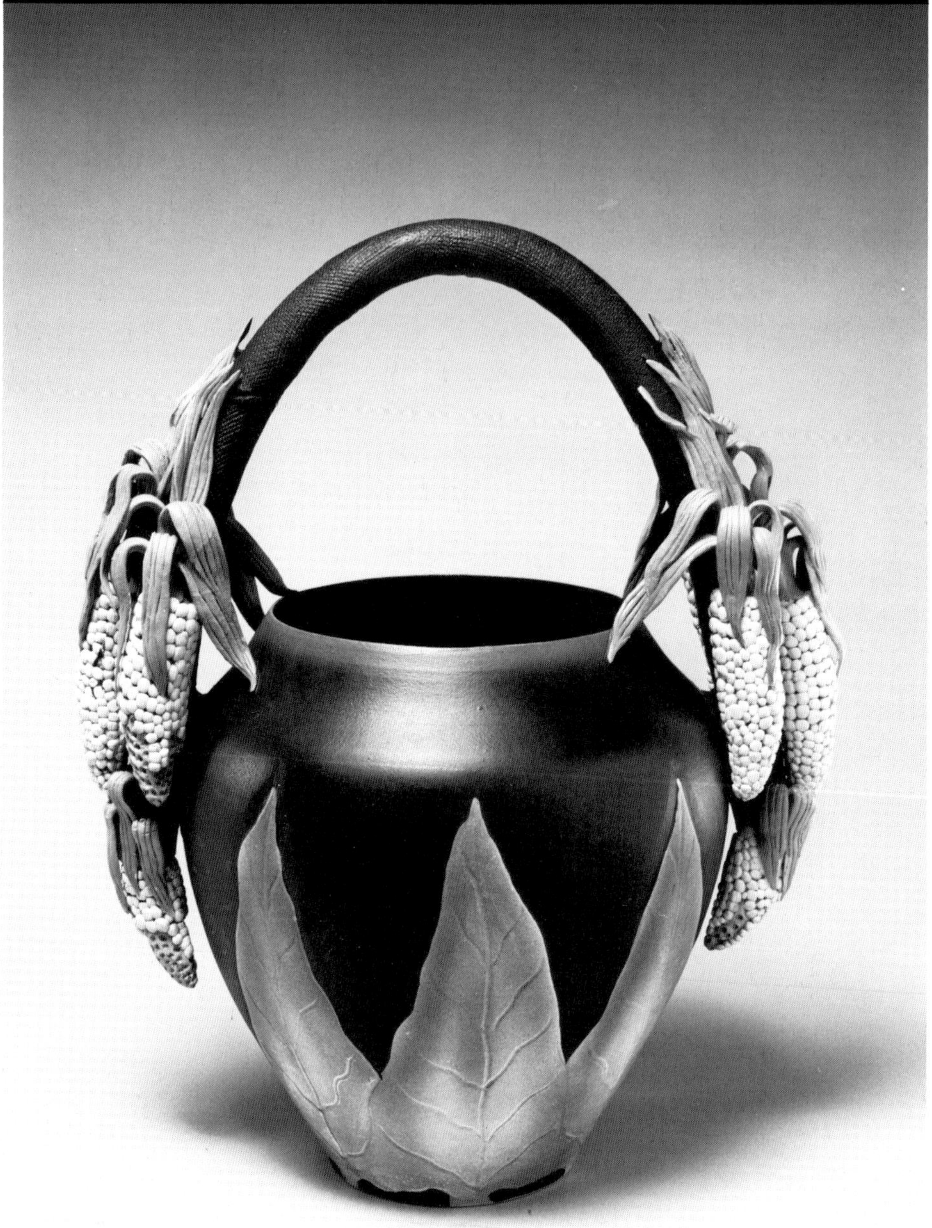

NANCY ADAMS
Spirit Corn Vessel, 1986
earthenware
12 x 10 x 7½

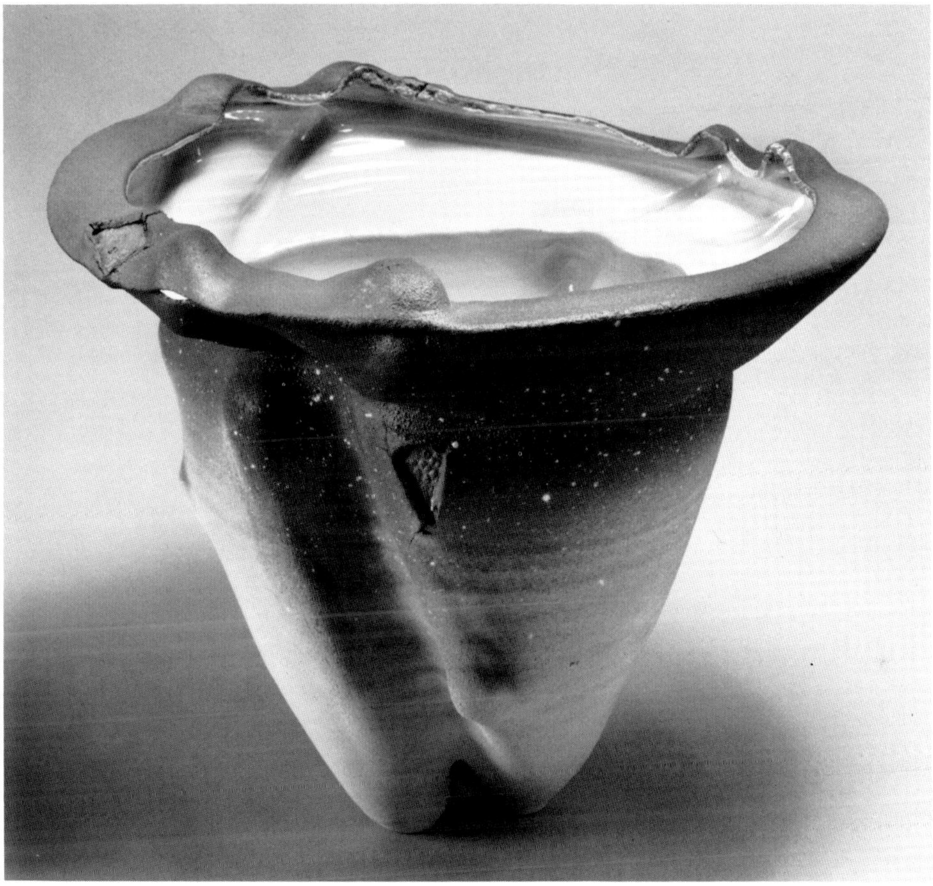

DOROTHY BAKER
Untitled, 1984
stoneware
12½ x 15 x 15

CURTIS AND SUZAN BENZLE
After You're Gone, 1986
porcelain
7 x 17 x 3

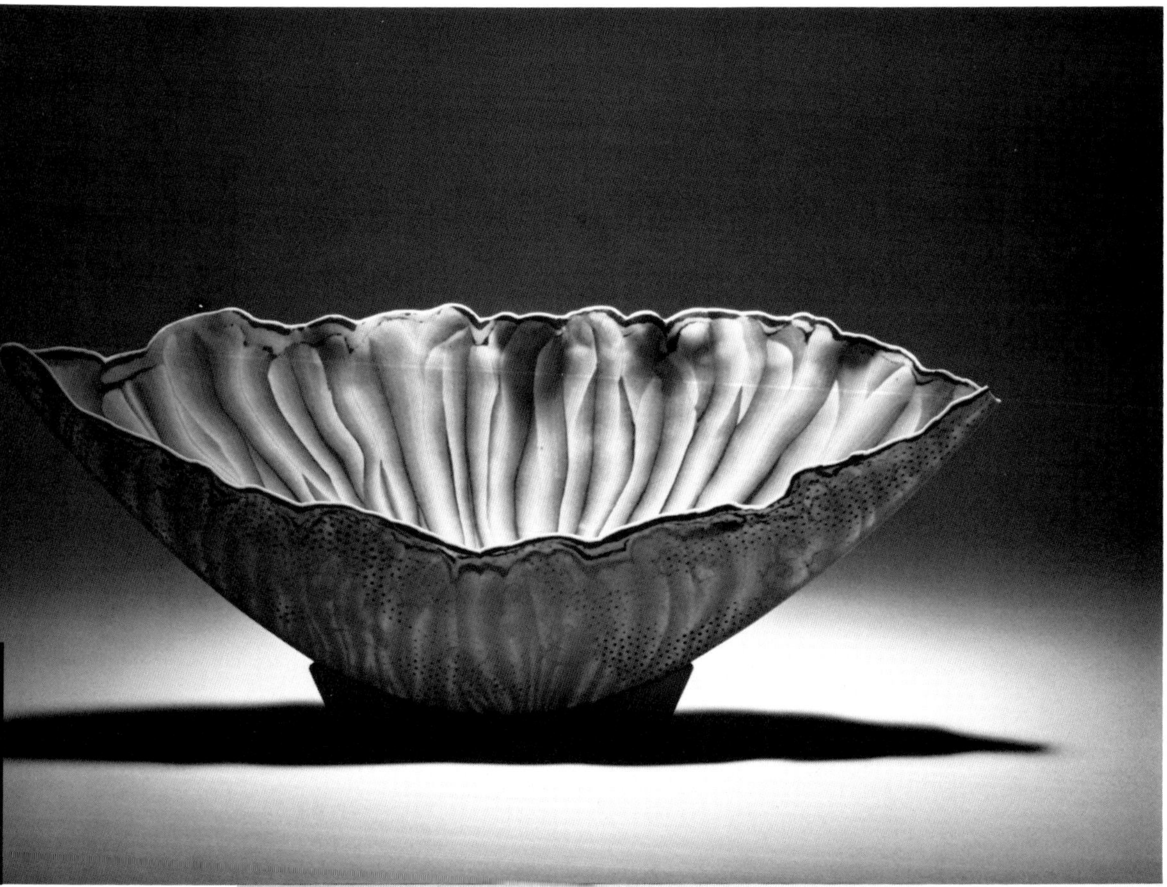

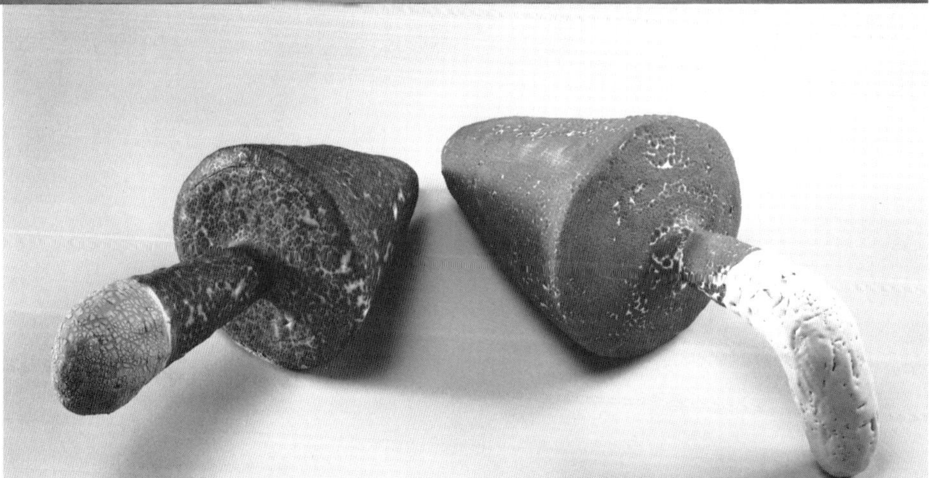

NINA BORGIA-ABERLE
Two Tops, 1986
earthenware
18 x 18 x 5

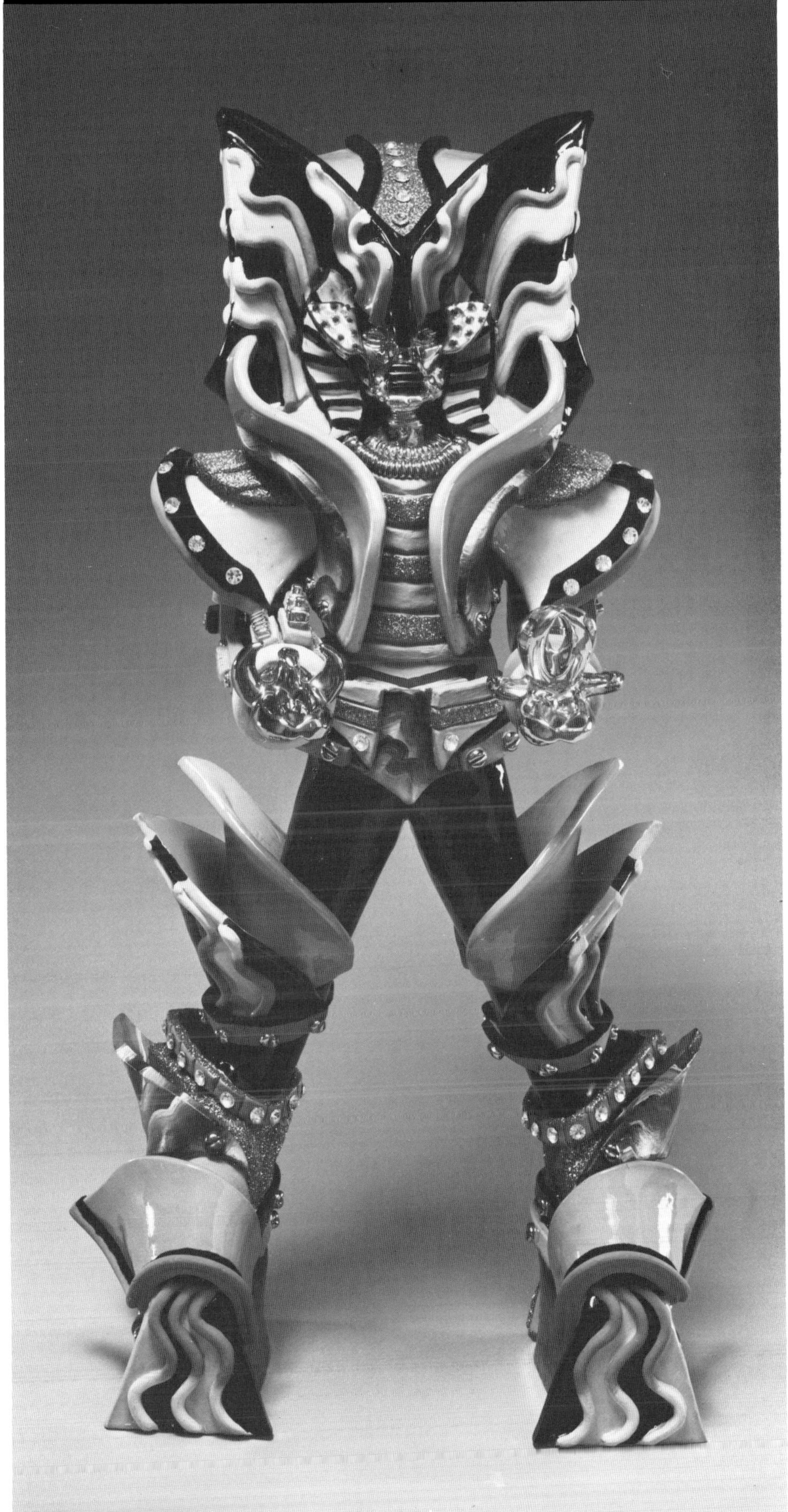

TOBY BUONAGURIO
Streamline Robot, 1985
earthenware
23 x 15 x 12

JIM CASWELL
Ma Tante Pandore, 1986
earthenware
10 x 15 x 24

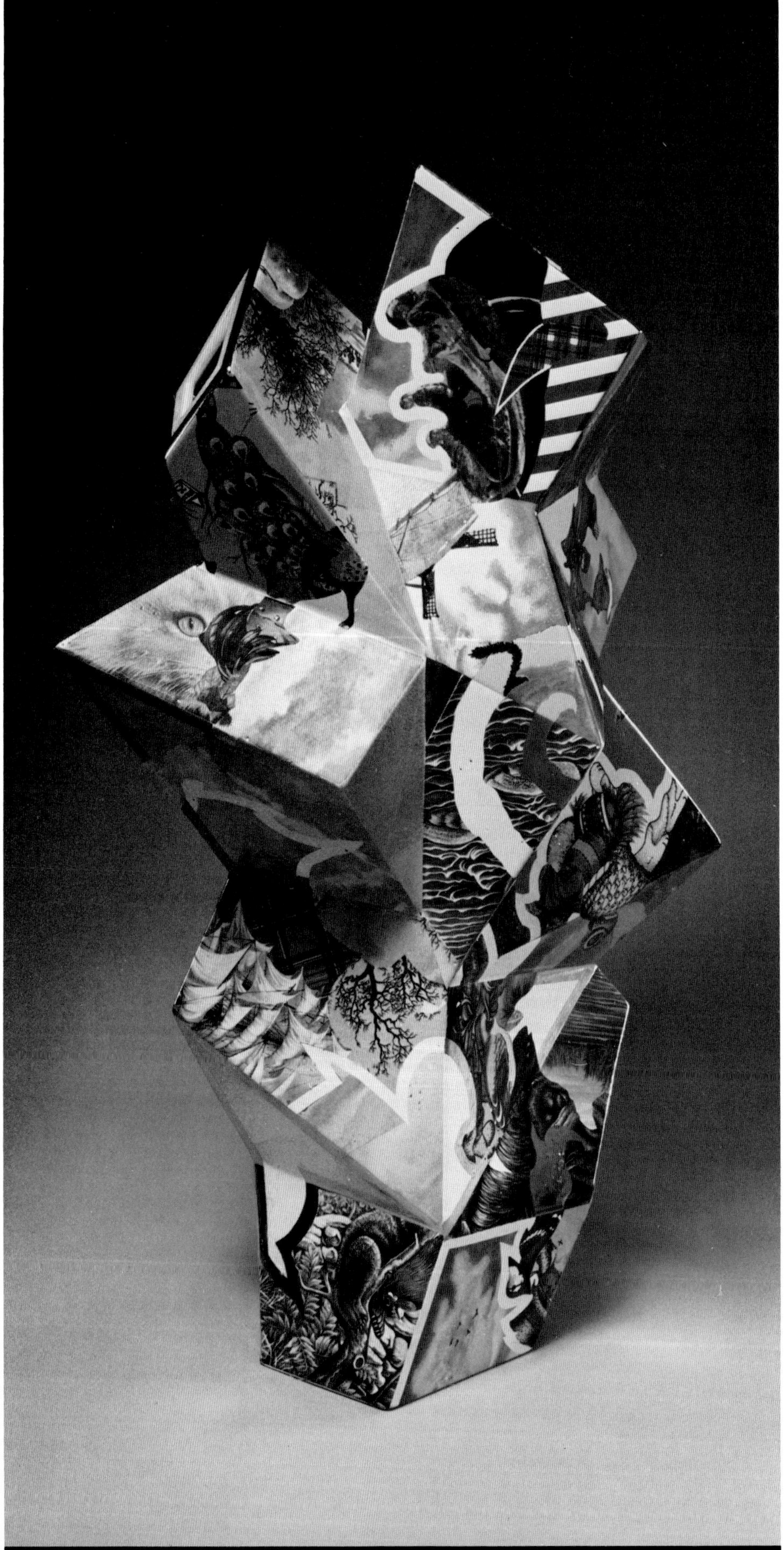

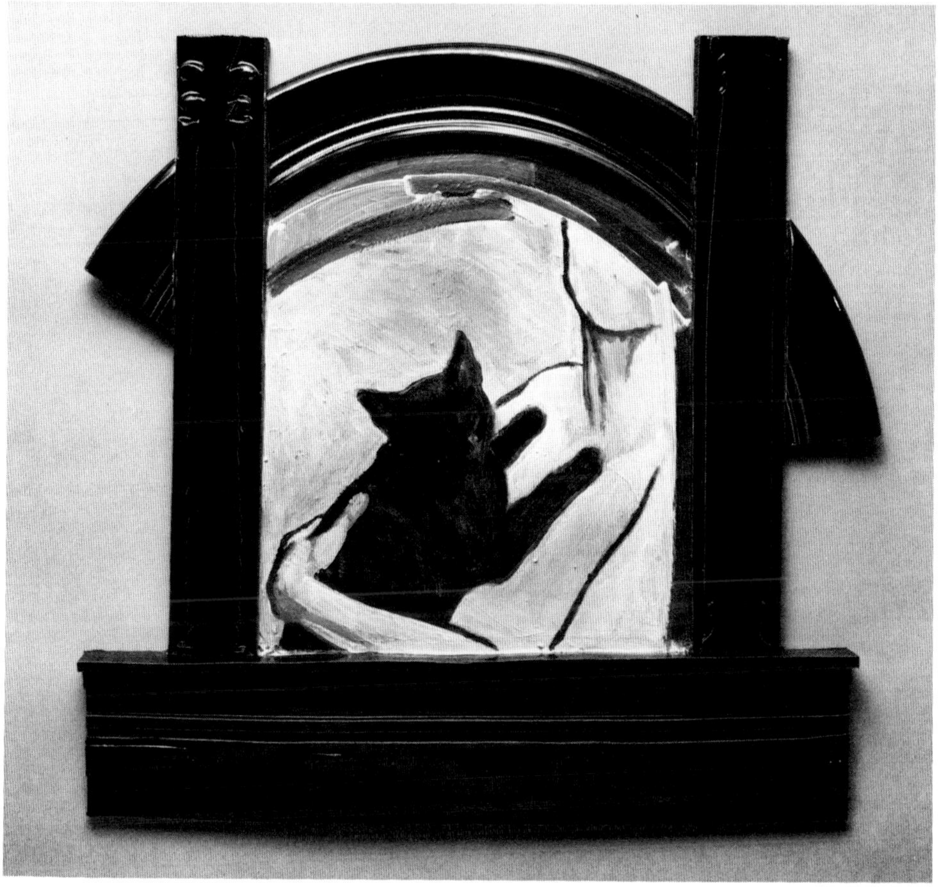

BETH CHANGSTROM
Blackie Turns Green,
1986
earthenware
28 x 28 x 2

SCOTT CHAMBERLIN
Untitled, 1986
earthenware
84 x 60 x 22

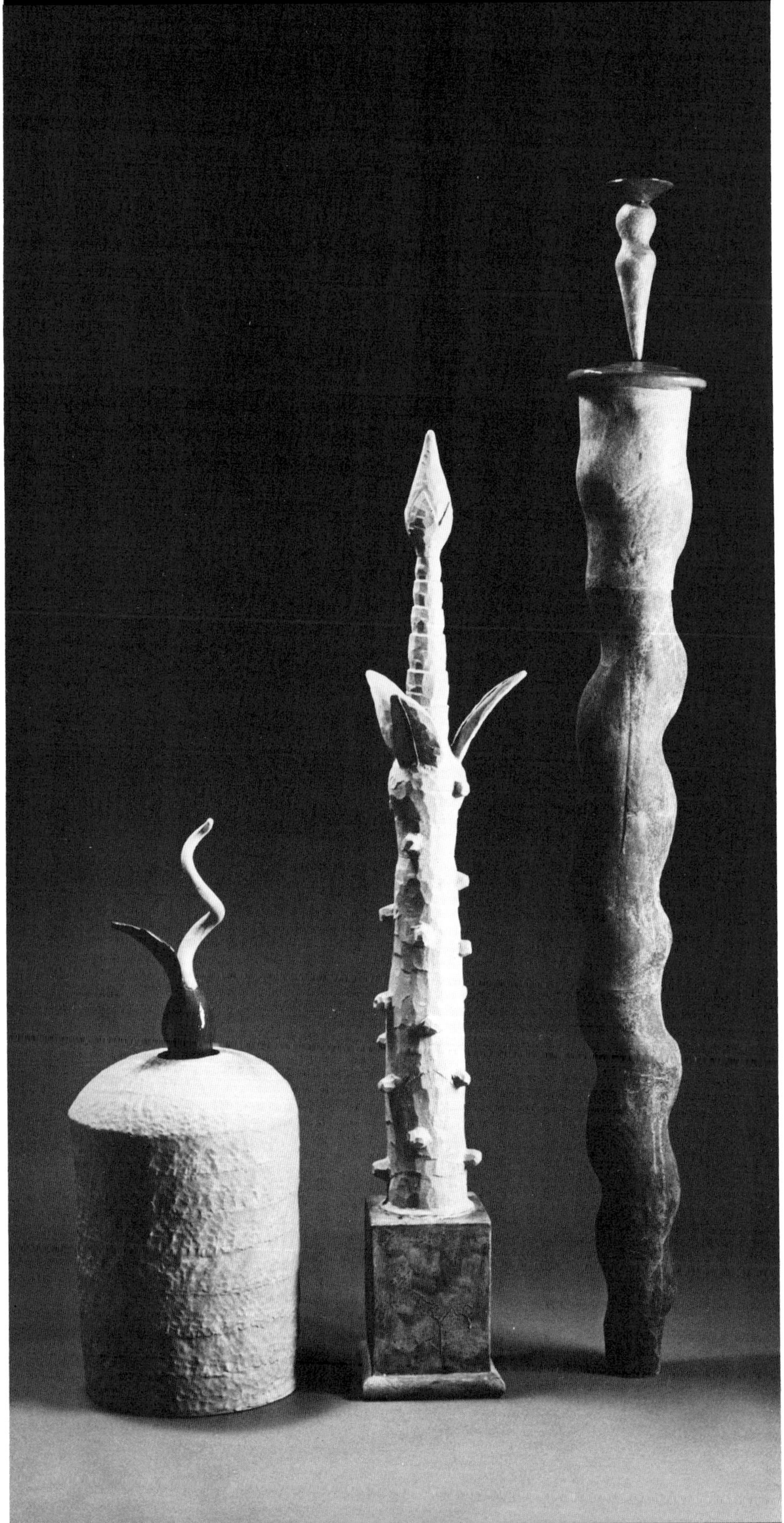

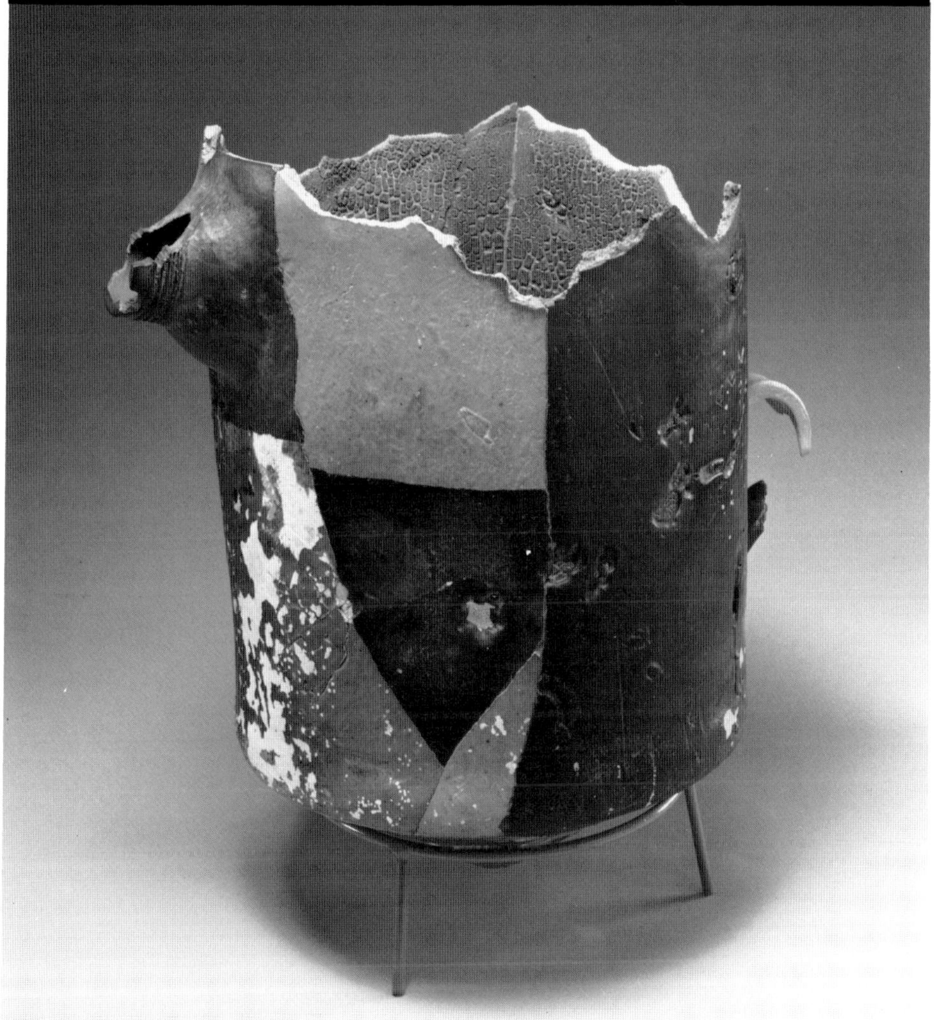

PATRICK S. CRABB
Relic Dispenser, 1986
earthenware, metal
16½ x 10½ x 10½

ANNE CURRIER
Réciproque, 1986
earthenware
29 x 22 x 9

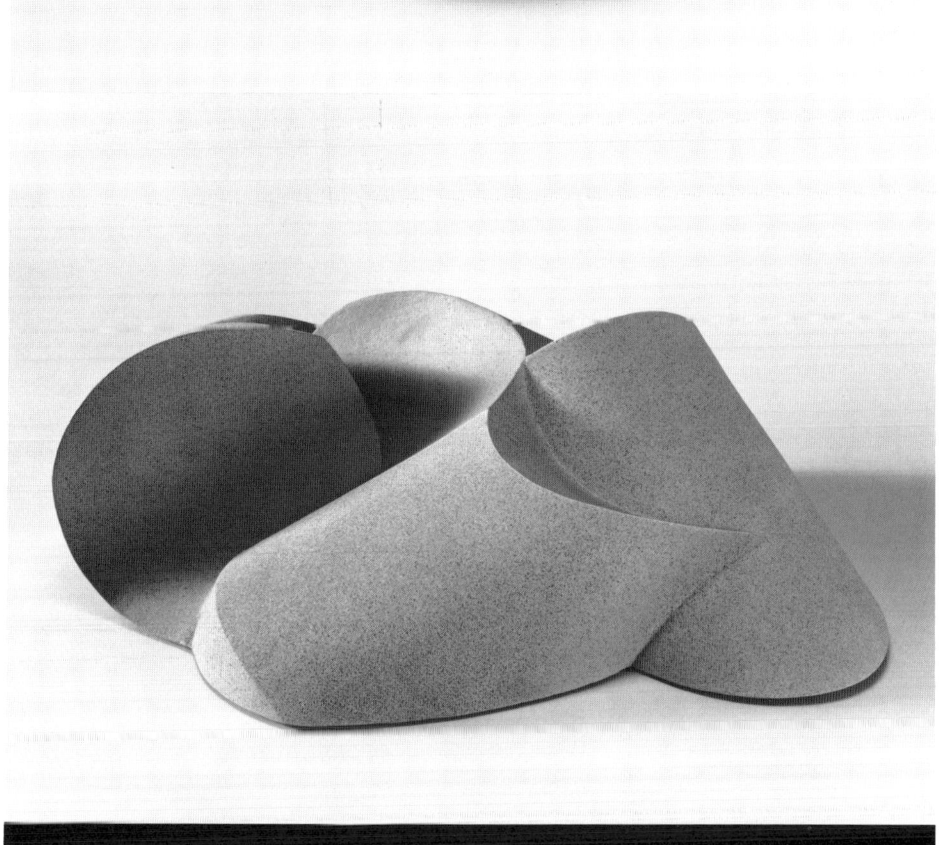

ROSELINE DELISLE
Triptyque 6, 1986
porcelain
21 x 6¾ diam.

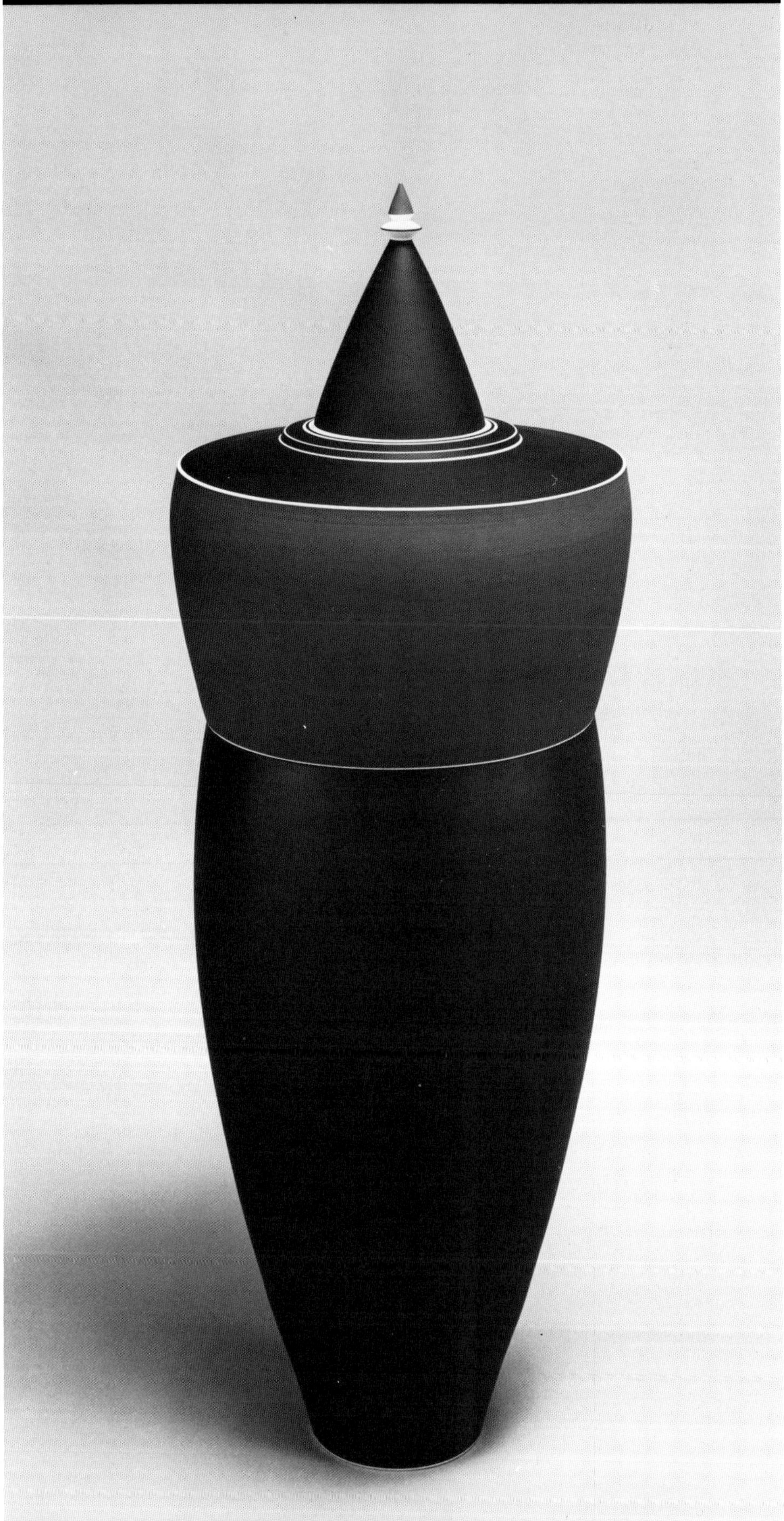

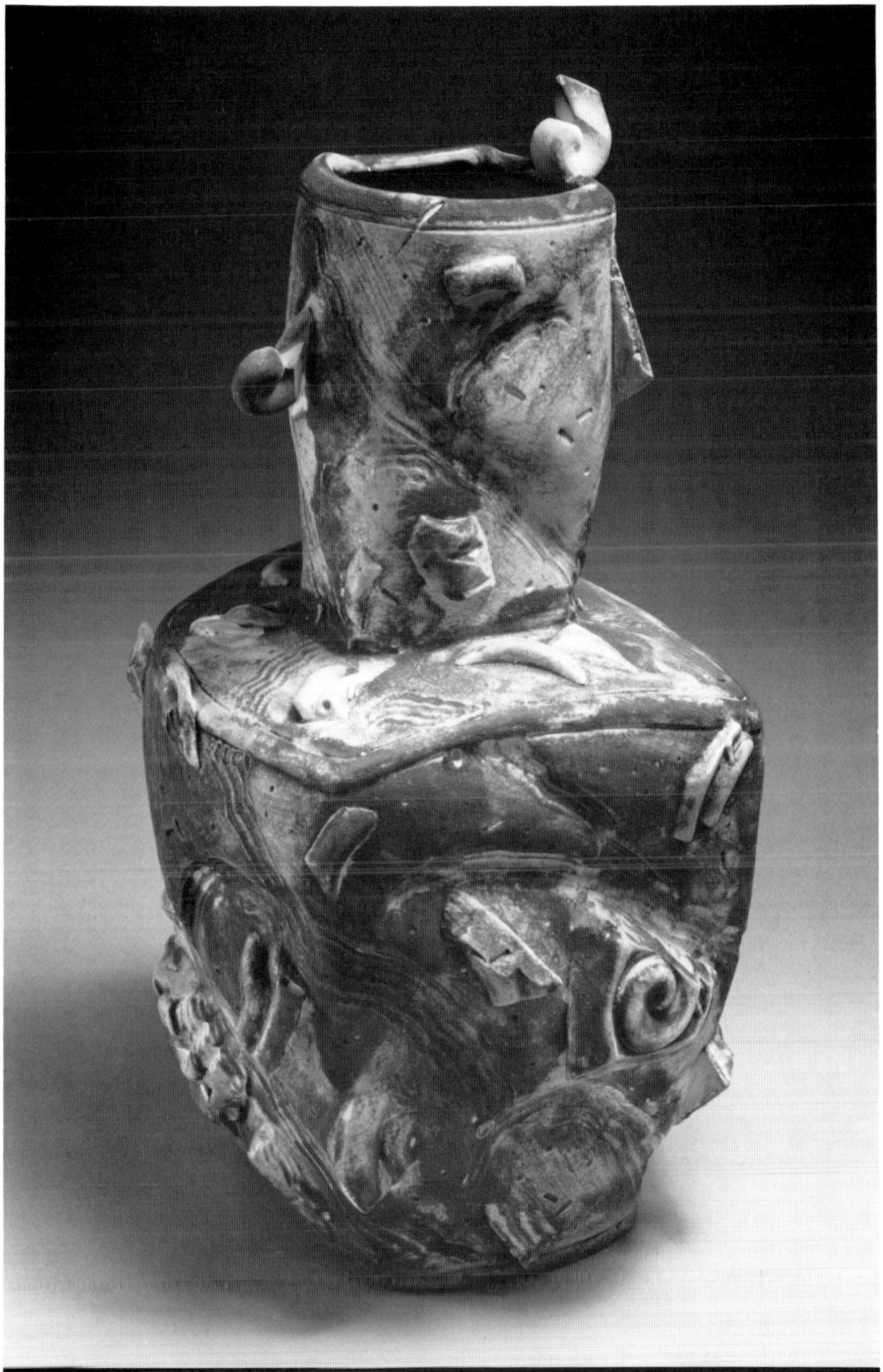

MARK DERBY
Blue Vase, 1986
stoneware
20 x 6 x 9

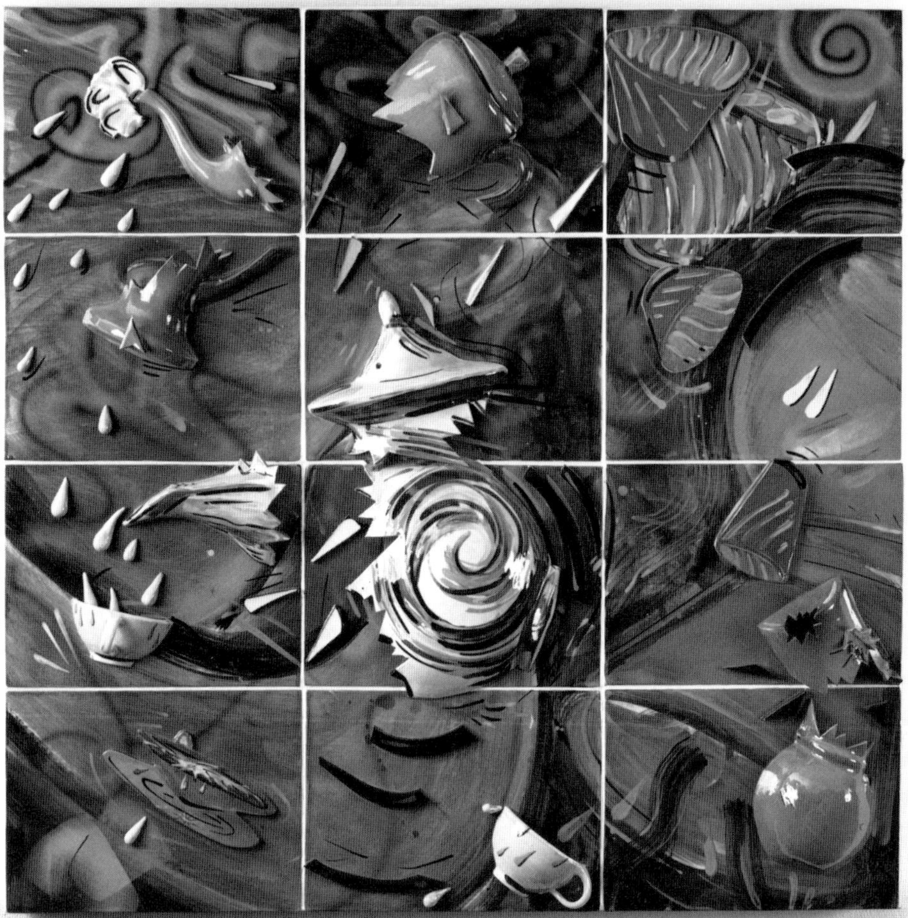

STEVEN DONEGAN
Break with Tradition,
1986
earthenware
43½ x 44½ x 7

PAUL A. DRESANG
Untitled, 1986
porcelain
7 x 8 x 4

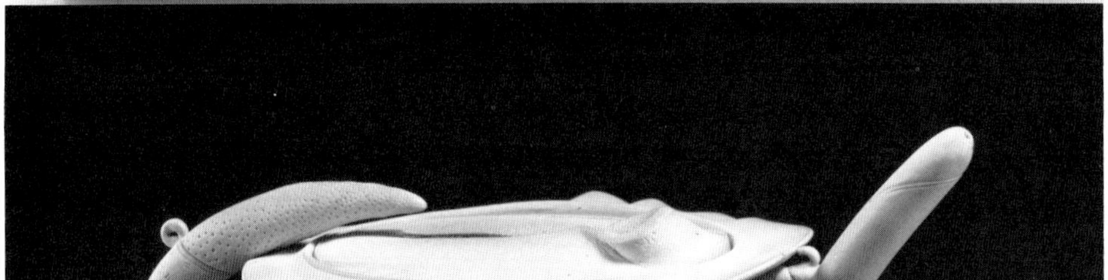

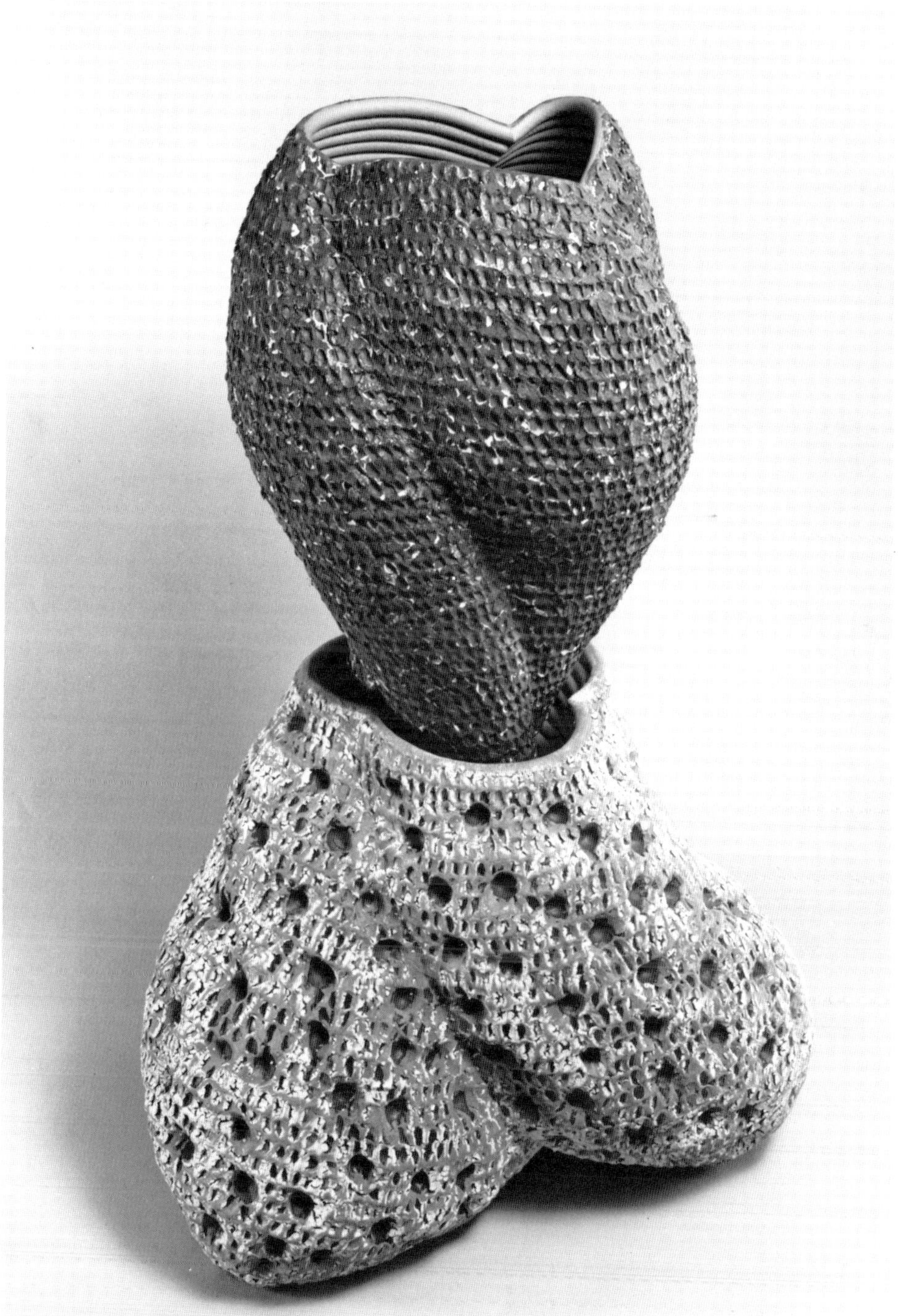

GARY ERICKSON
Stout Blue Spiral, 1986
earthenware
38 x 24 x 24

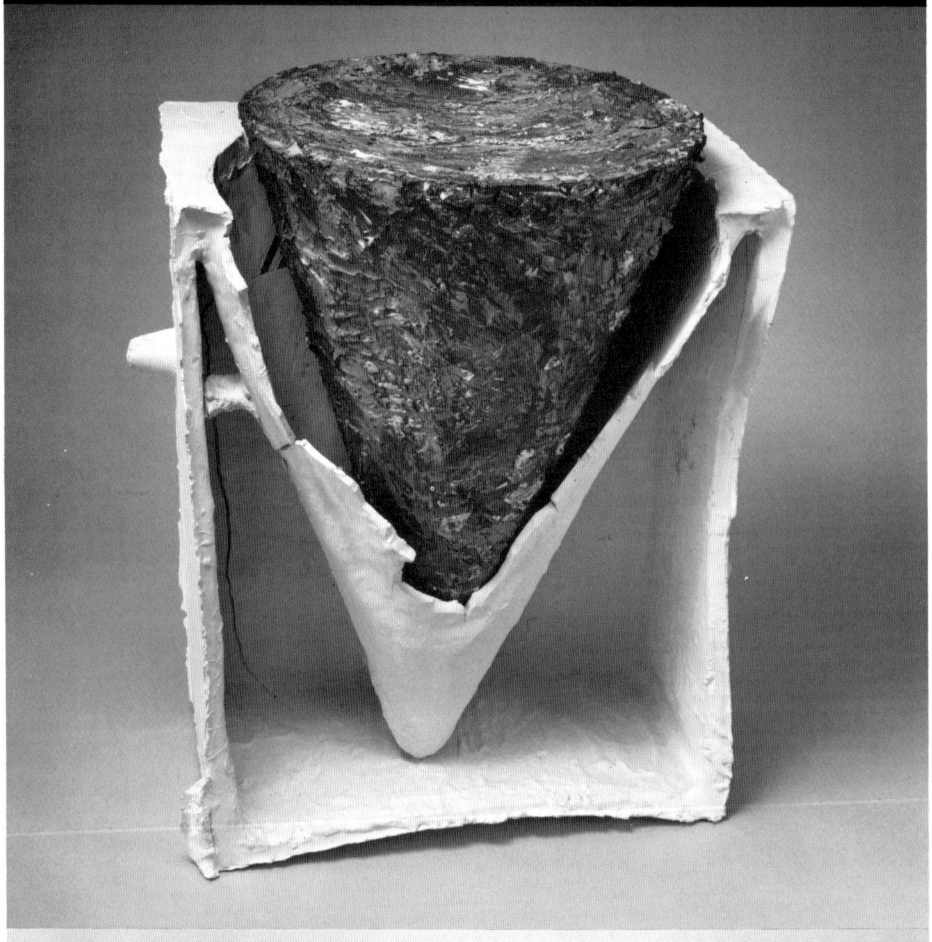

RON FONDAW
Birth Cone, 1985
porcelain
27 x 20 x 13

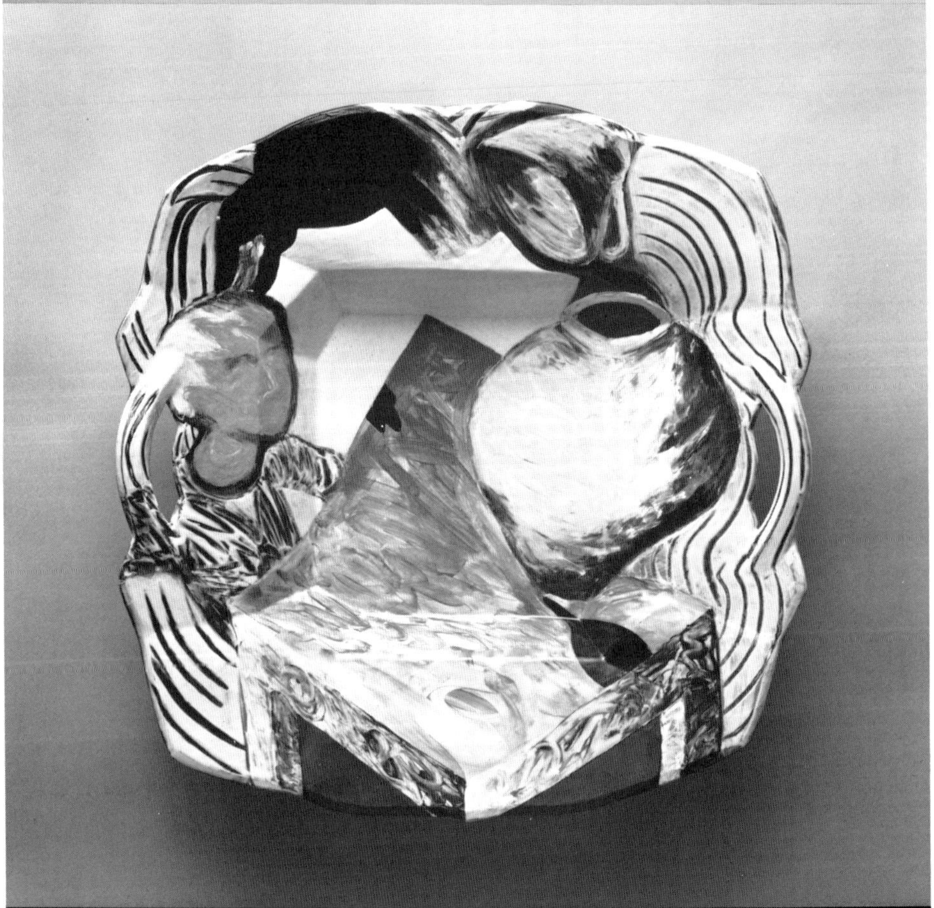

JOHN FRANTZ
Untitled, 1986
earthenware
25 x 25 x 6

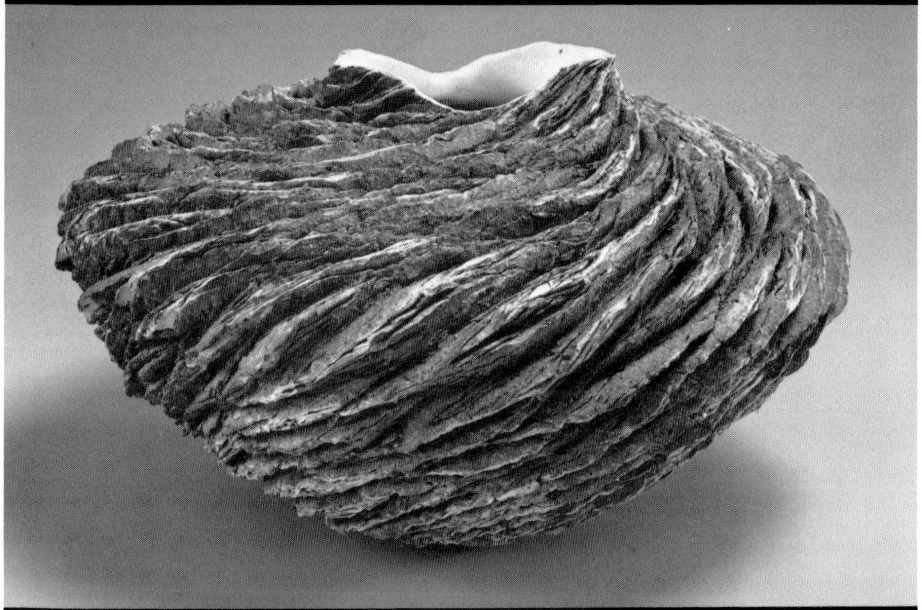

ANNE GOLDMAN
Stone Flower Vase, 1986
stoneware
14 x 18 diam.

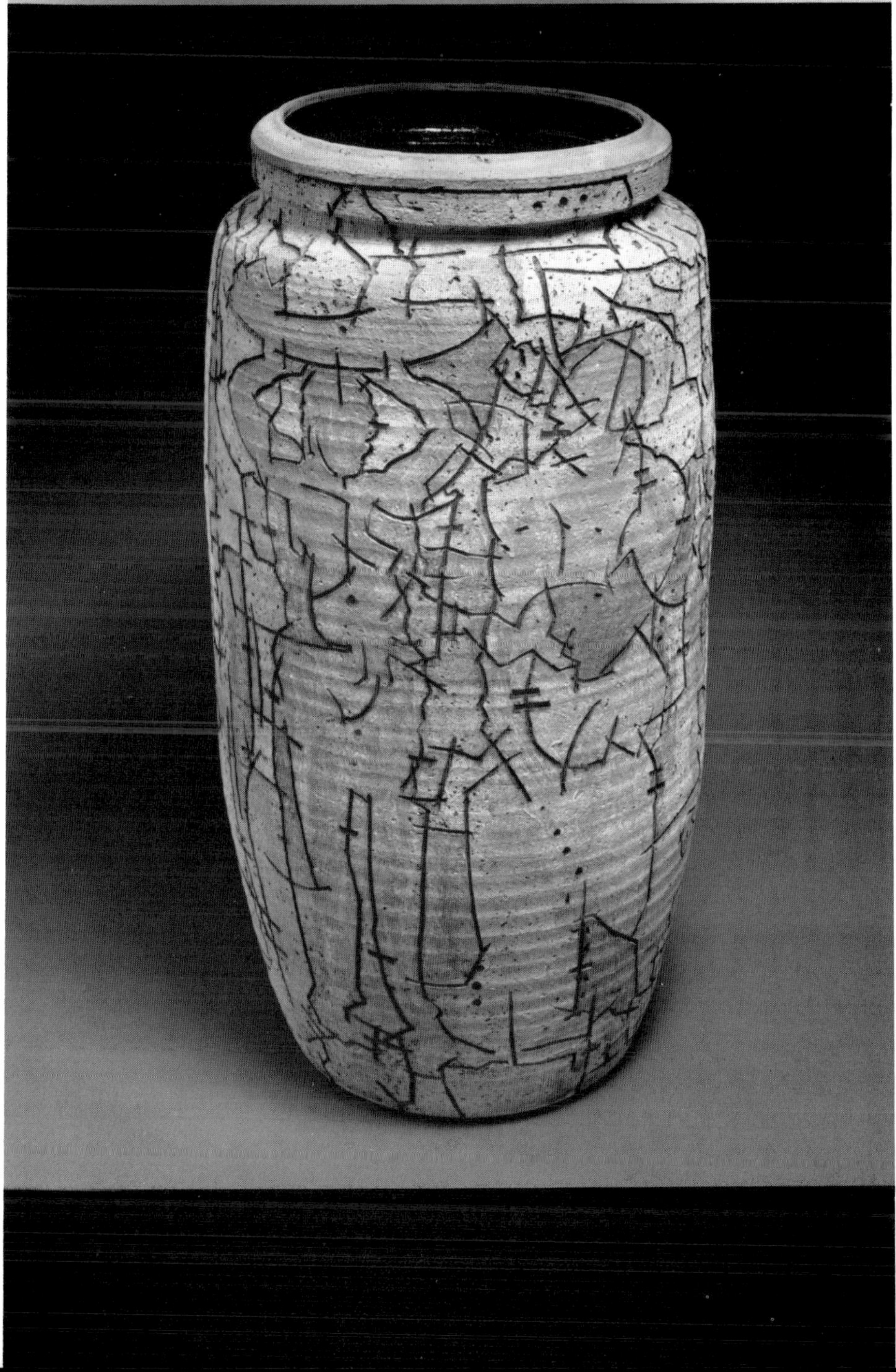

MICHAEL GUBKIN
An Insatiate Ingrate, 1986
stoneware
21 x 11 x 10

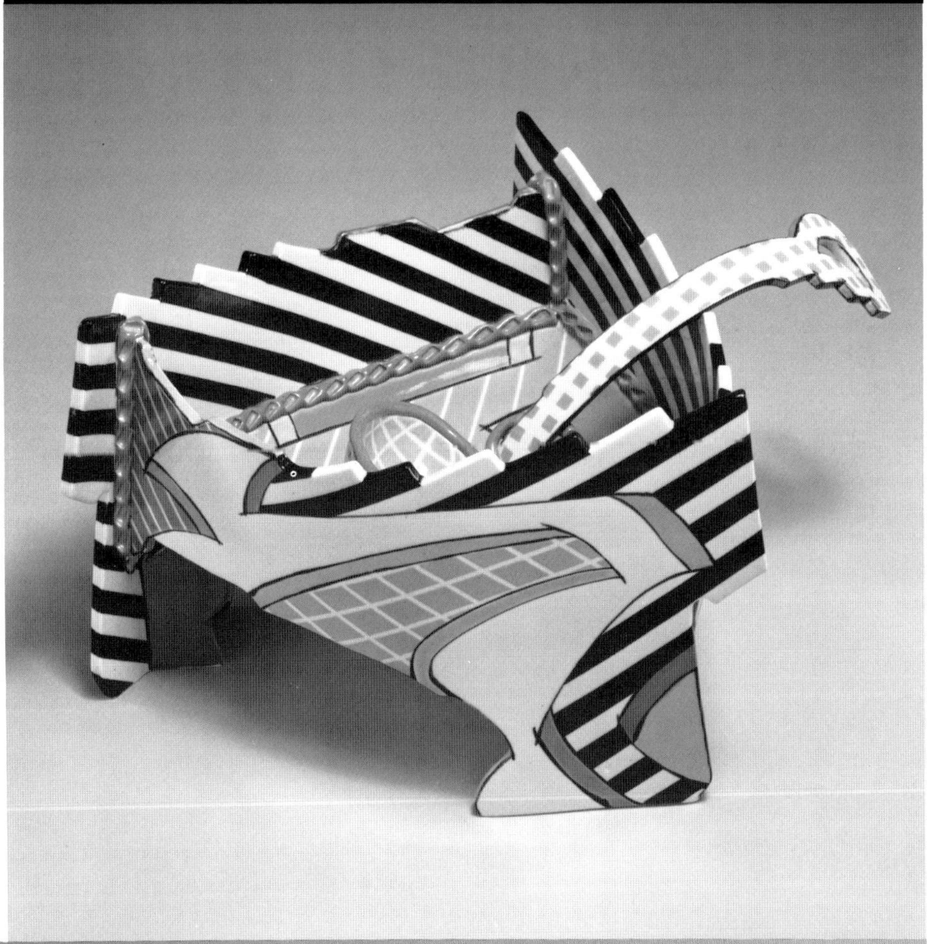

DOROTHY HAFNER
Gazpacho Server II,
1986
porcelain
Server: 8 x 11½ x 11½
Ladle: 11 long

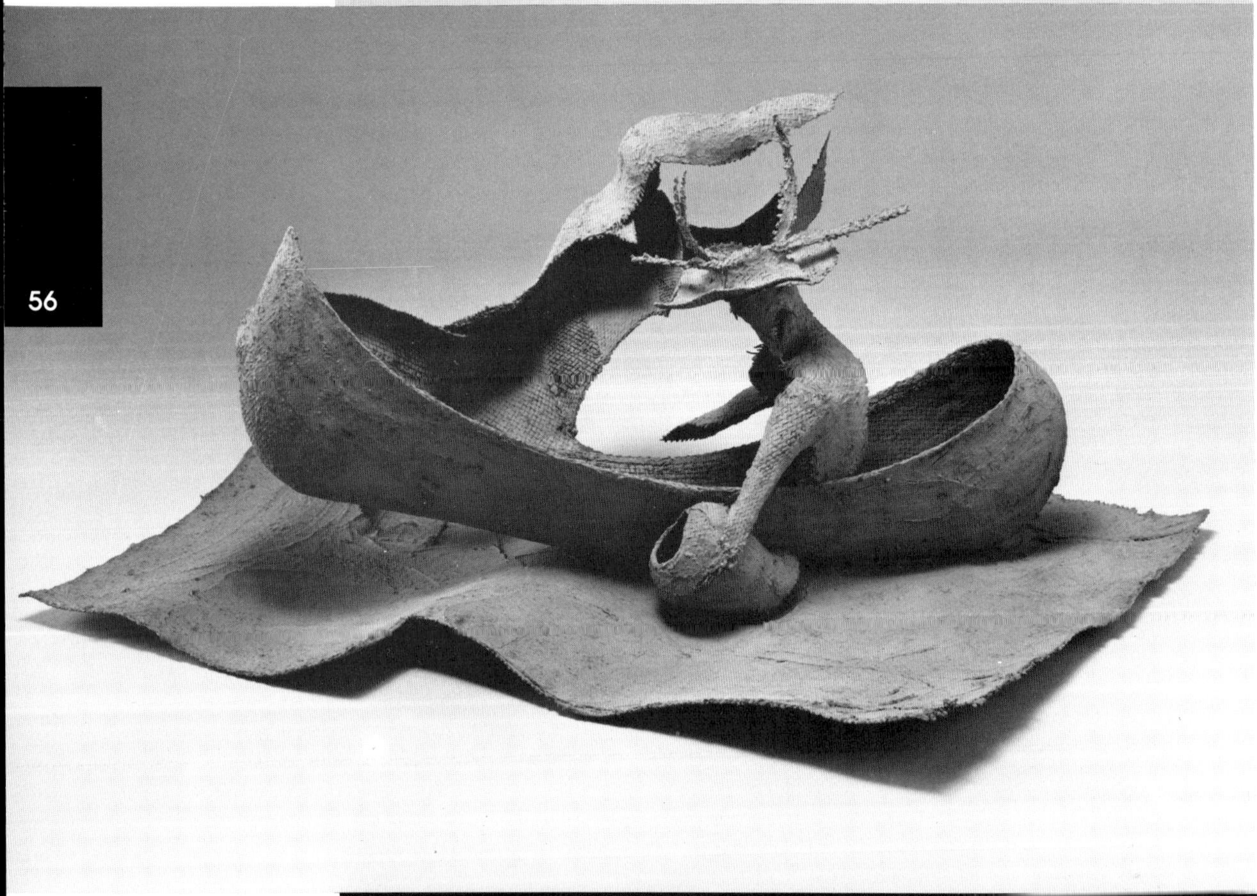

WALTER HALL
Incident at Sea, 1986
earthenware, steel
24 x 21 x 13

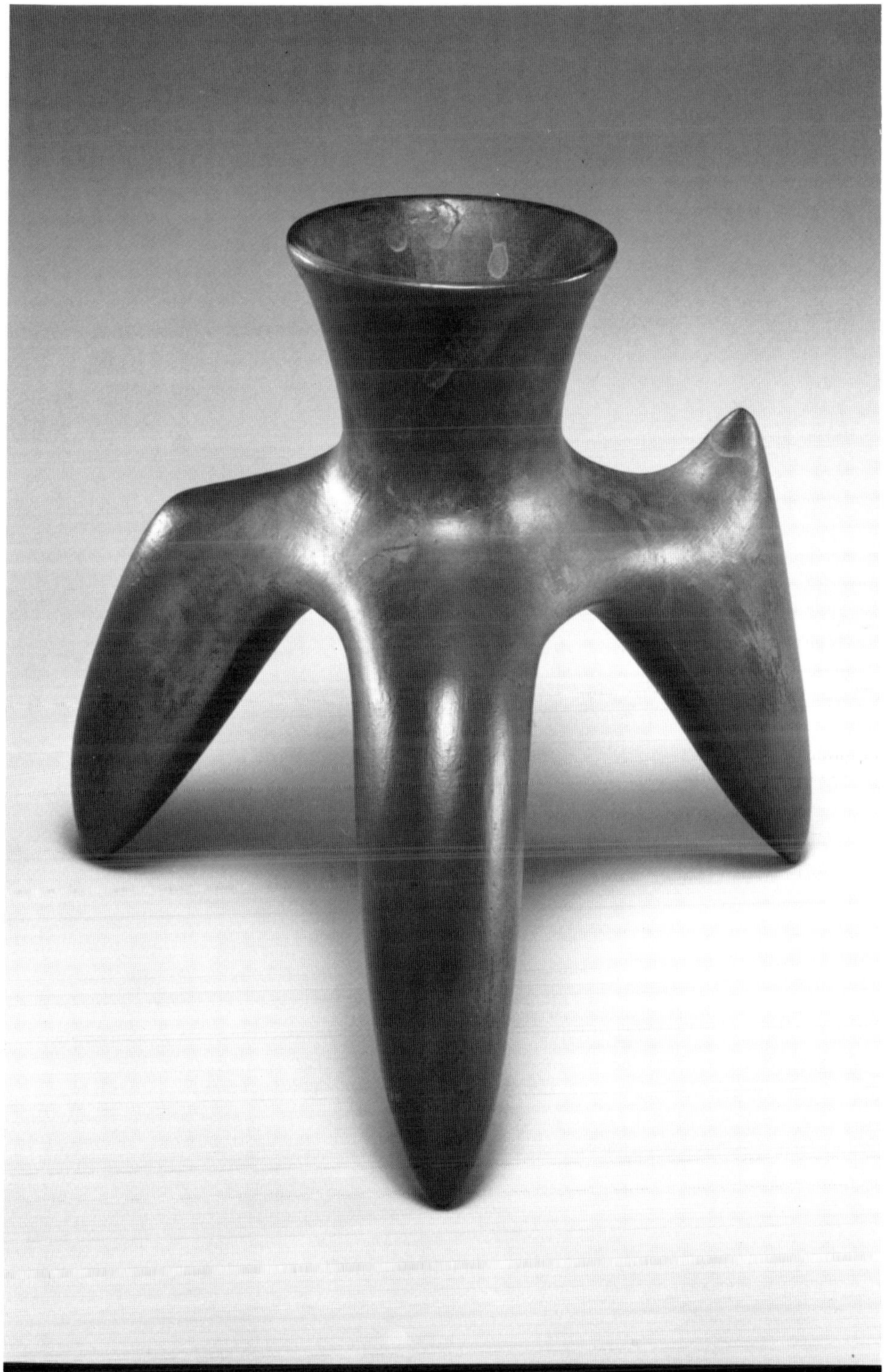

RICHARD HIRSCH
Ceremonial Cup #26,
1985-86
stoneware
12 x 12½ x 12

ABBY HUNTOON
Black Vase
with Pedestal, 1985
earthenware
50 x 18 x 19

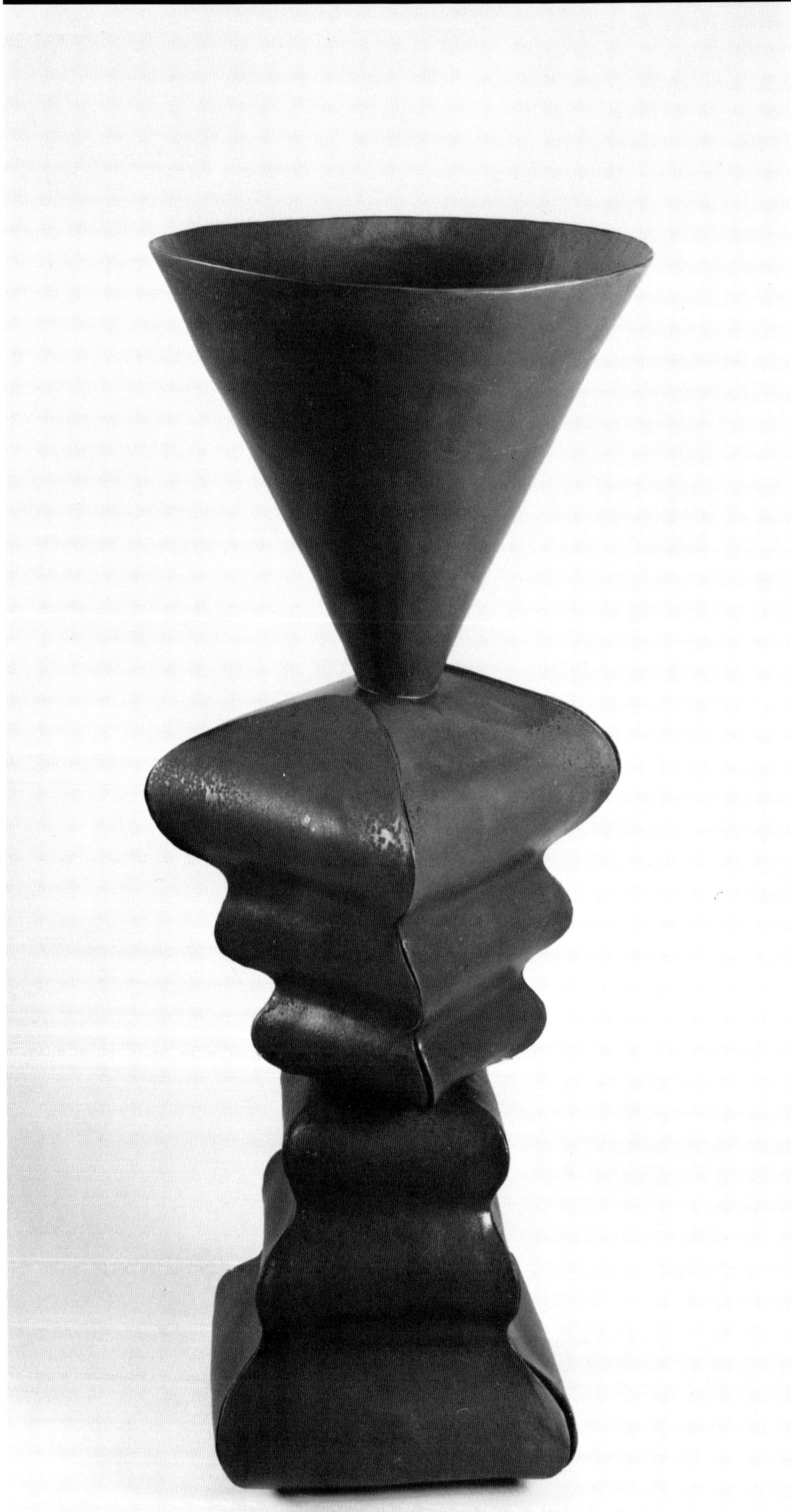

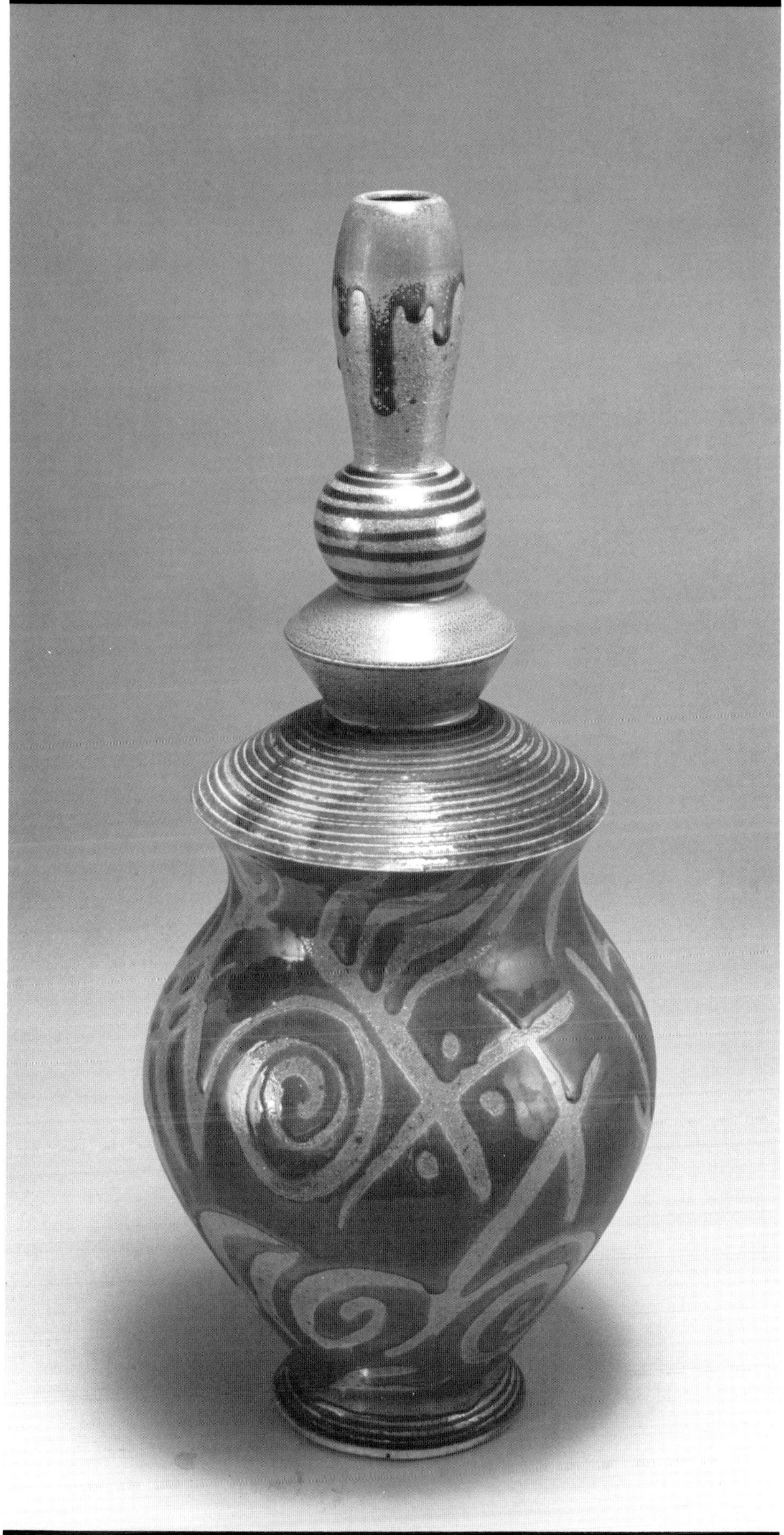

MARK D. JOHNSON
Vase, 1986
stoneware
20 x 9 diam.

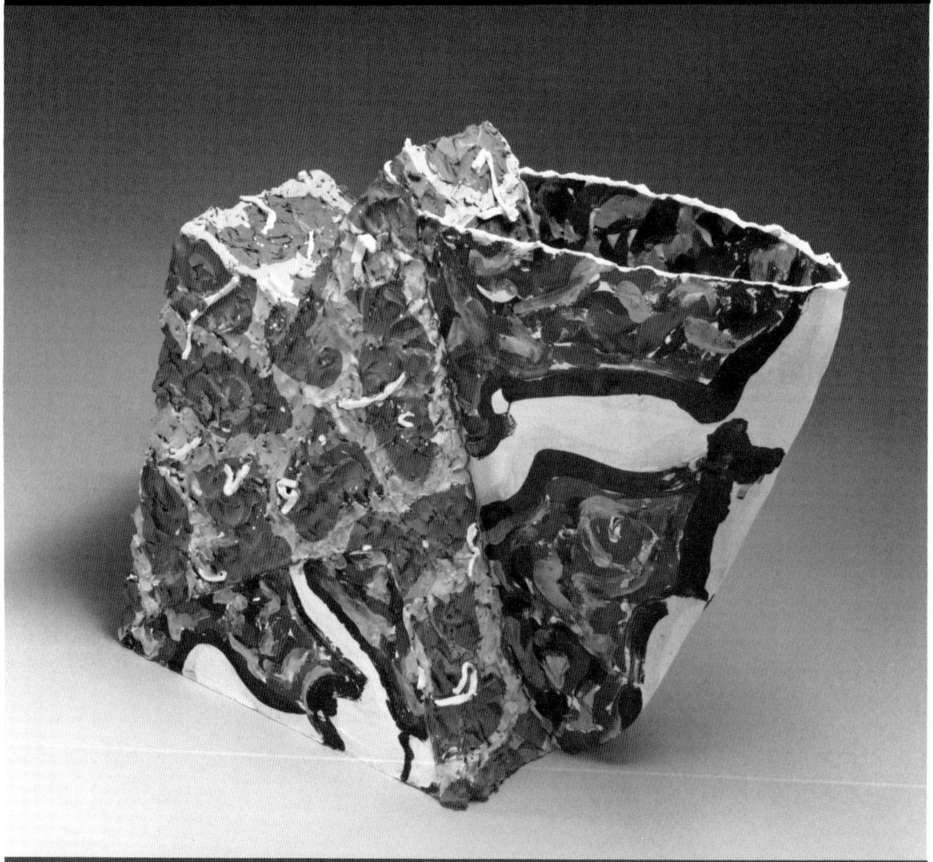

JAMES KLUEG
Arbor, 1986
earthenware
13 x 18 x 8

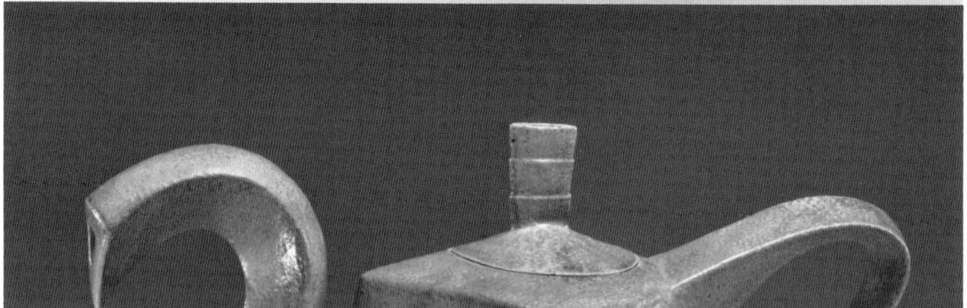

JAMES LAWTON
Teapot with Overcoat,
1985
earthenware
10 x 10 x 4

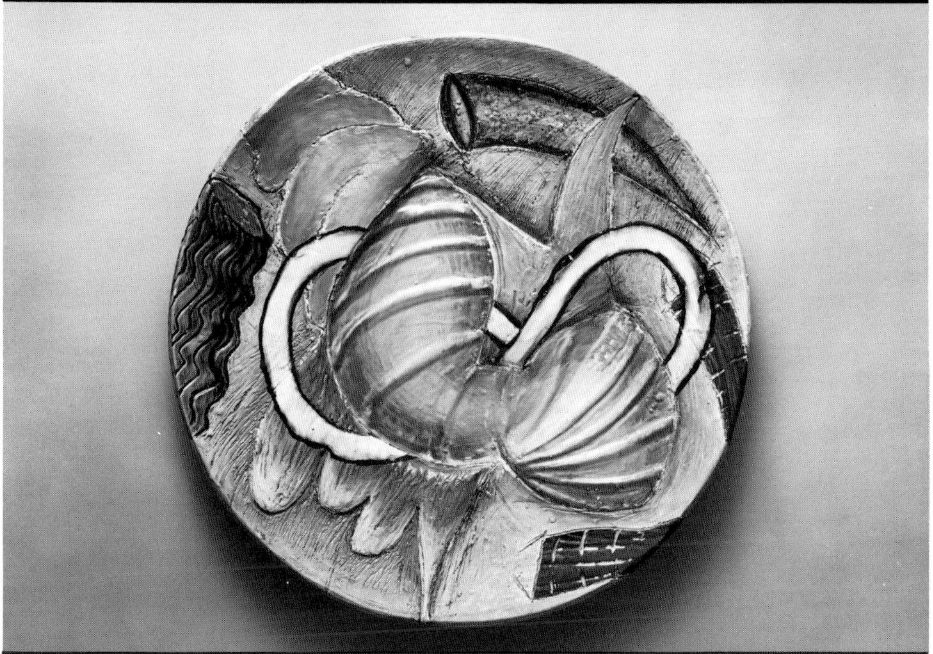

PATRICK LOUGHRAN
Untitled Plate, 1986
earthenware
3½ x 24 diam.

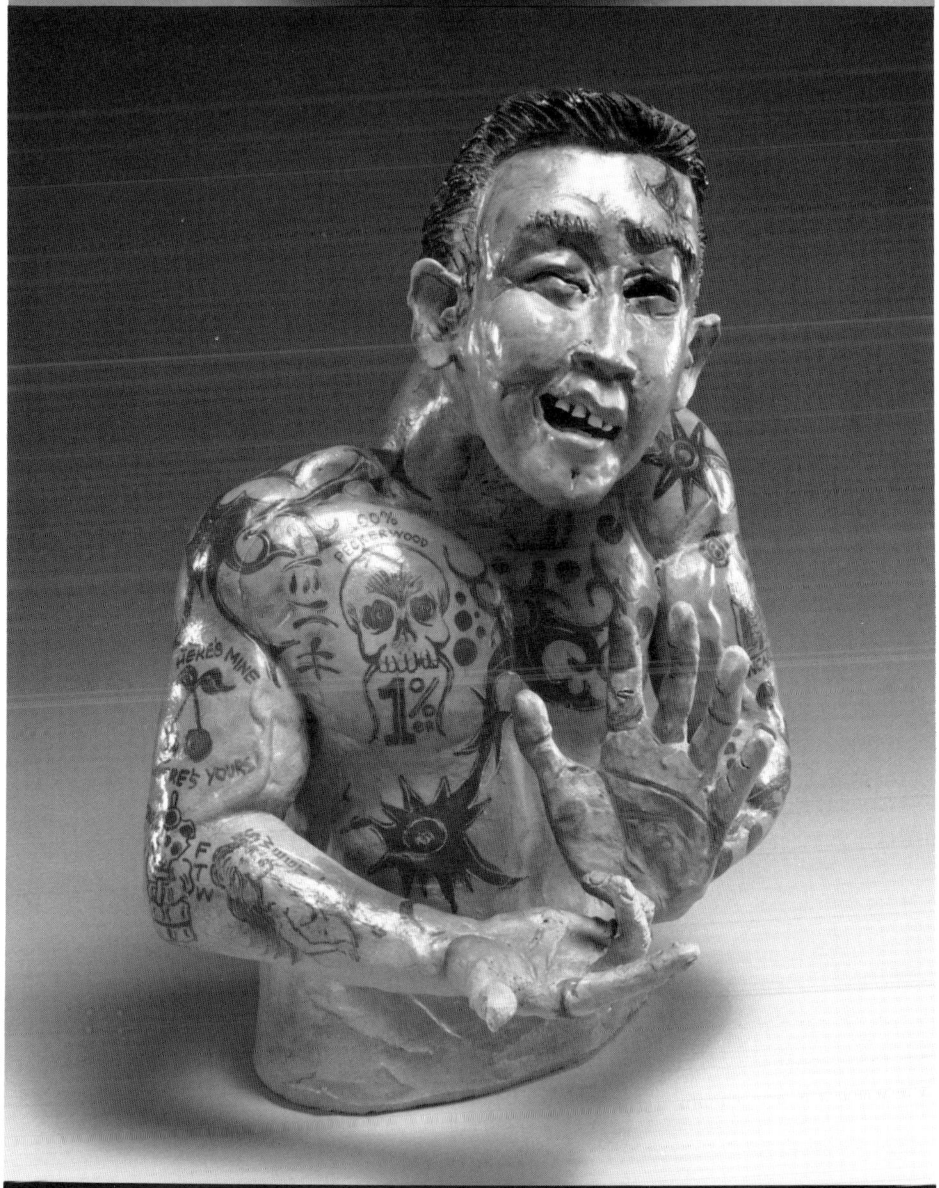

JOE MARISCAL
Doing a Nickel and Change, 1984
earthenware
23 x 16 x 12

PAUL MATHIEU
The Order of Desires, 1986
porcelain
12¾ x 12¾ x 4¼

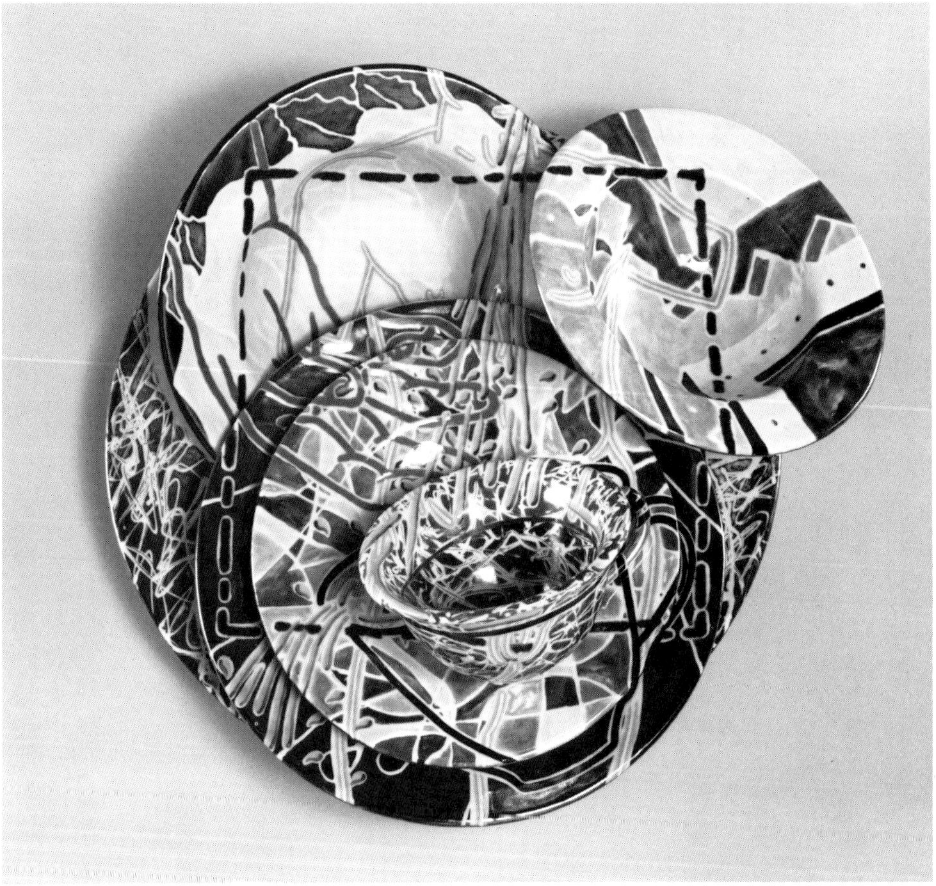

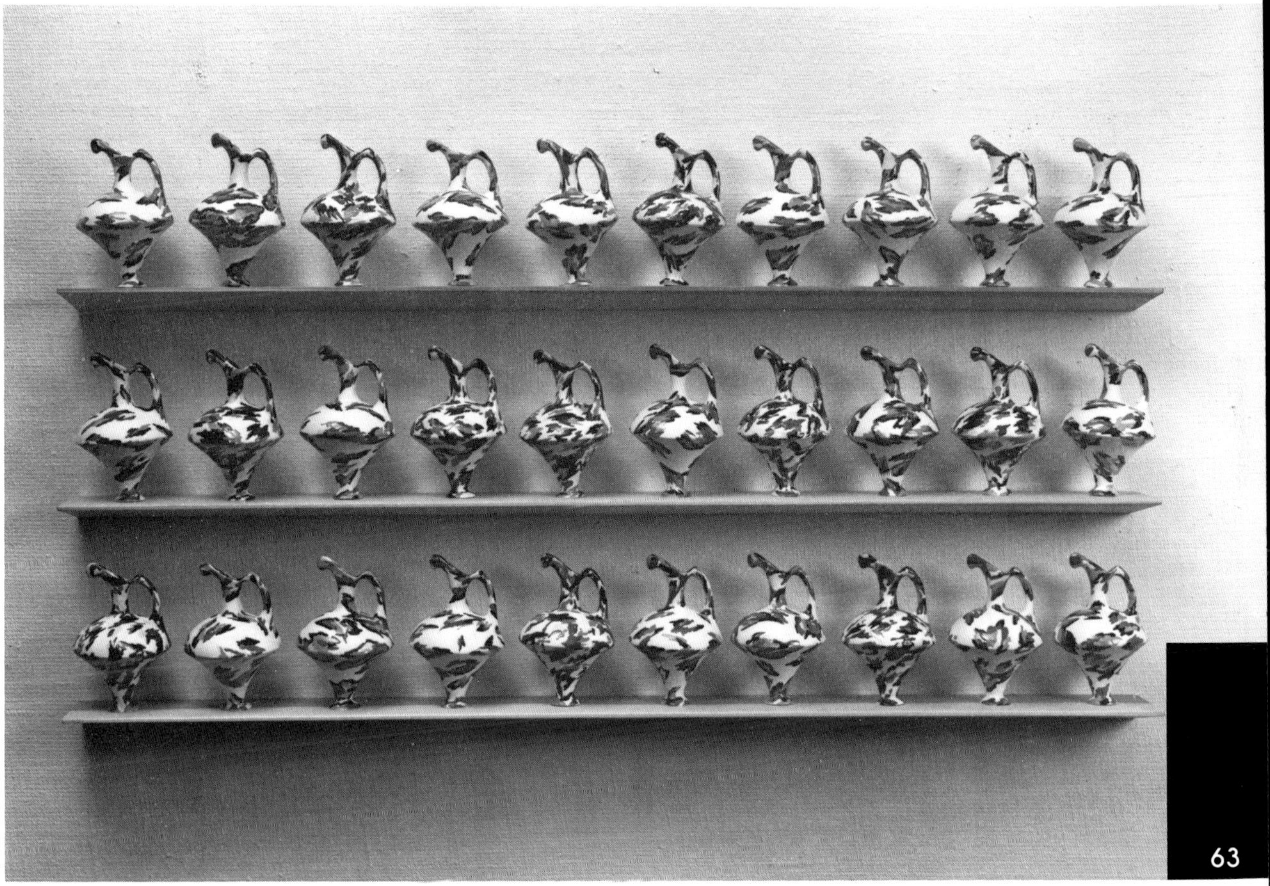

JUANITA JIMENEZ MIZUNO
Hittite Series #9, 1985
earthenware
24 x 36 x 5

JUDY MOONELIS
Woman in Bed II, 1986
earthenware
16 x 27 x 13

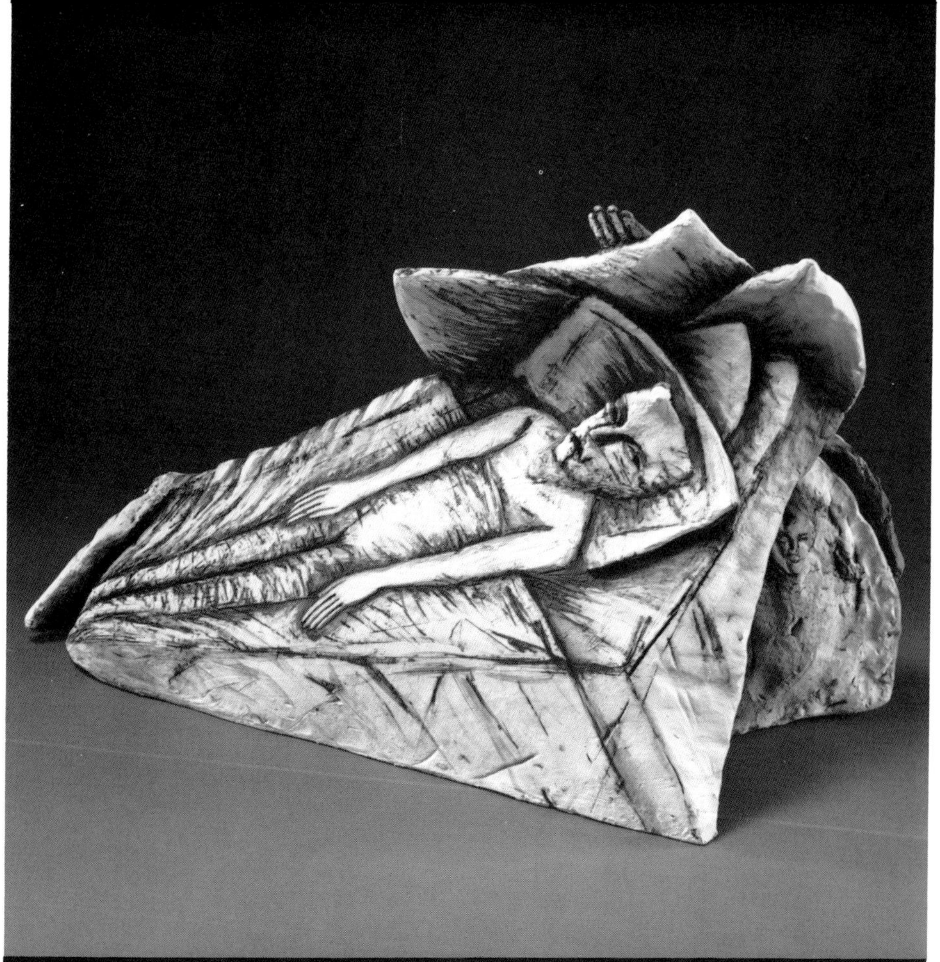

JANET NEUWALDER
Teapot, 1985
porcelain
13 x 20 x 12

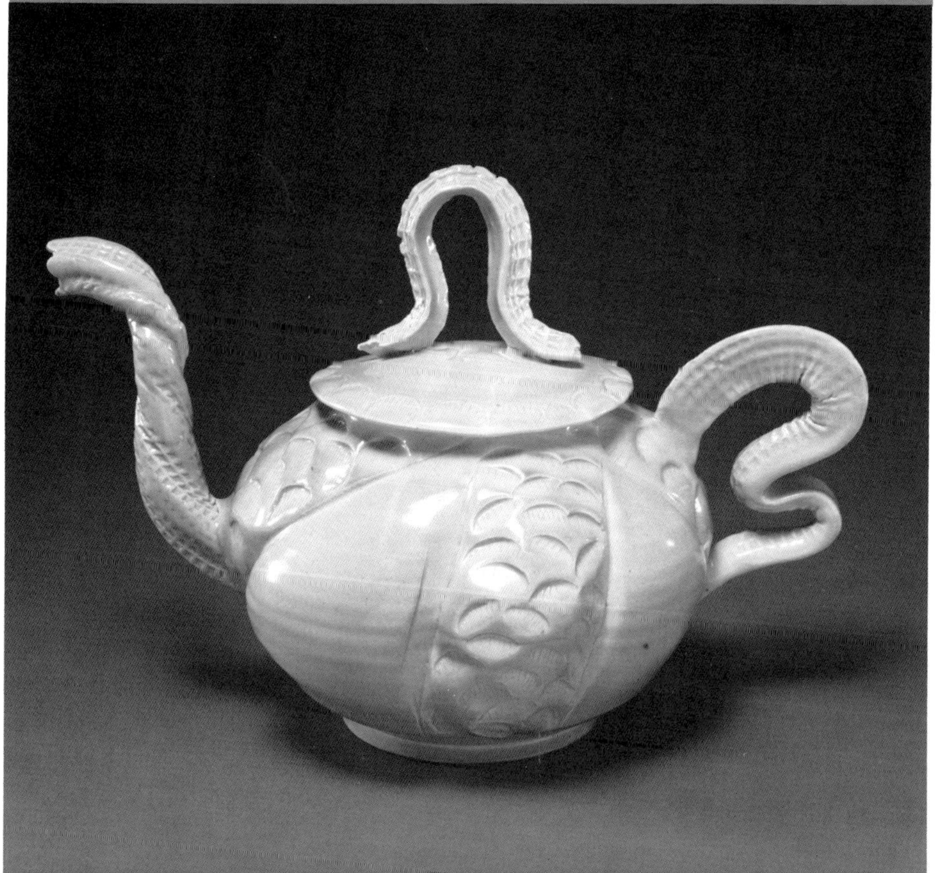

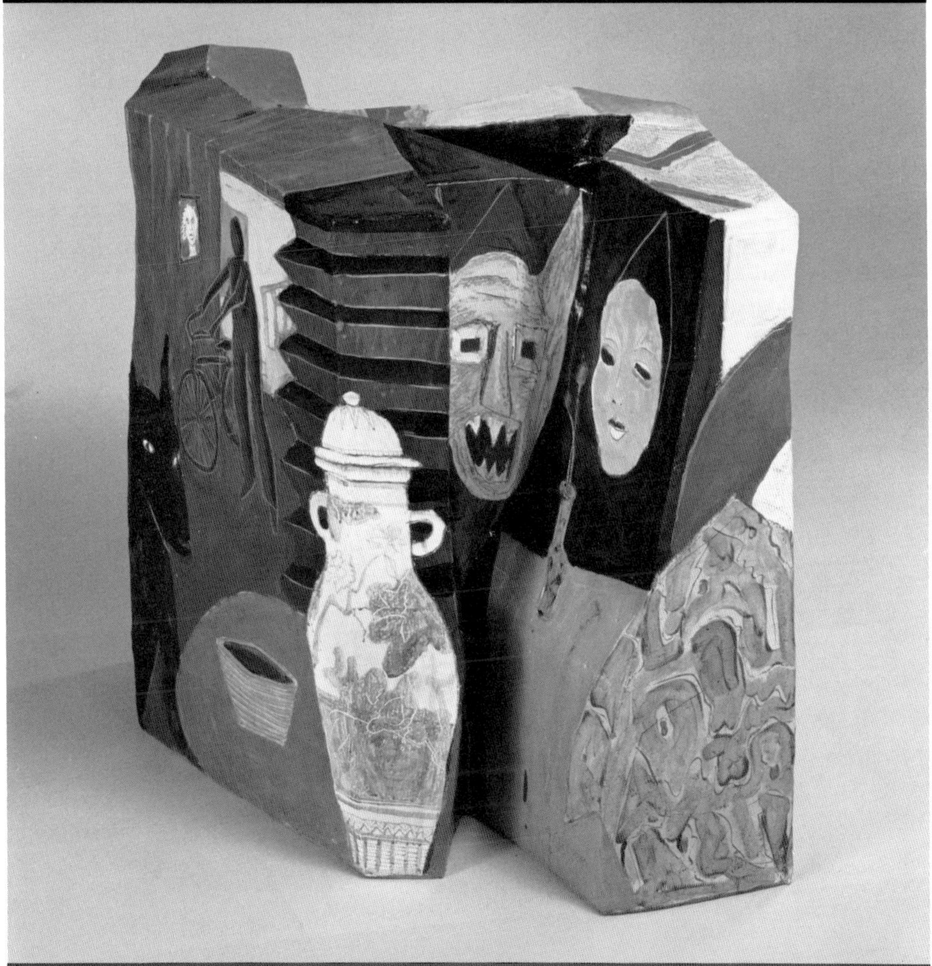

FRANK OZEREKO
Interior 6, 1986
earthenware
36 x 30 x 21

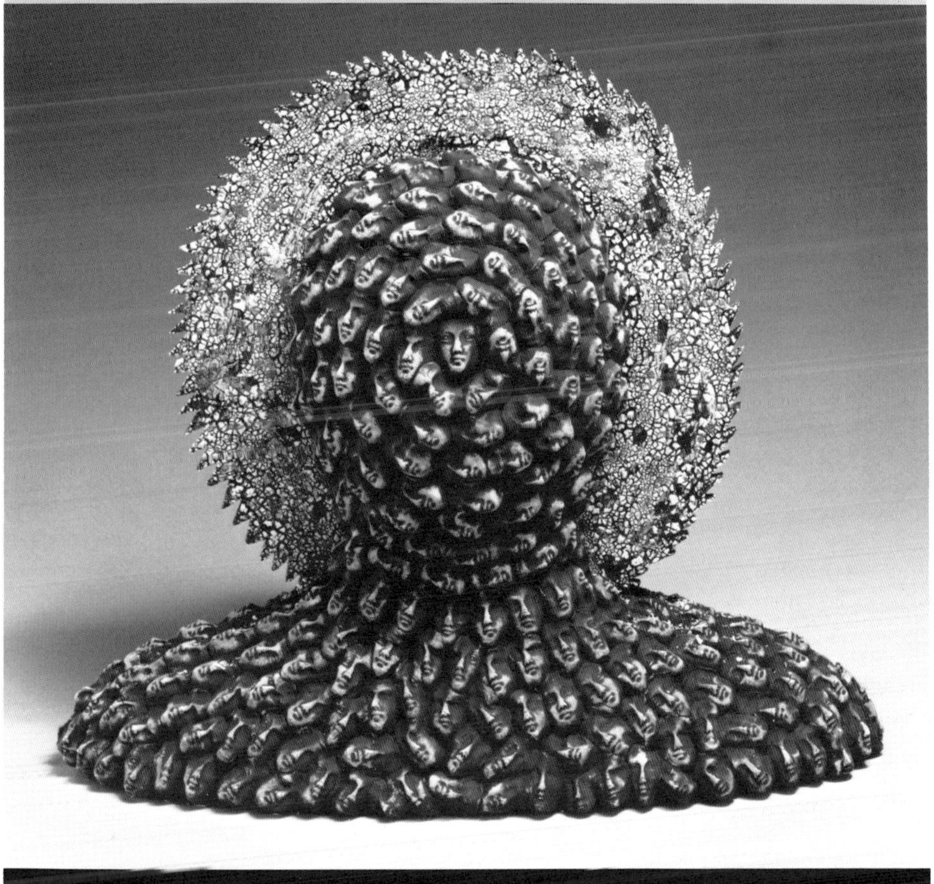

MARIO PETRIRENA
Black Madonnas Are Never Wasted on Benjamin Jones, 1986
earthenware
23 x 19 x 7

PATRICIA RIEGER
Sentinel, 1986
earthenware
60 x 38 x 21

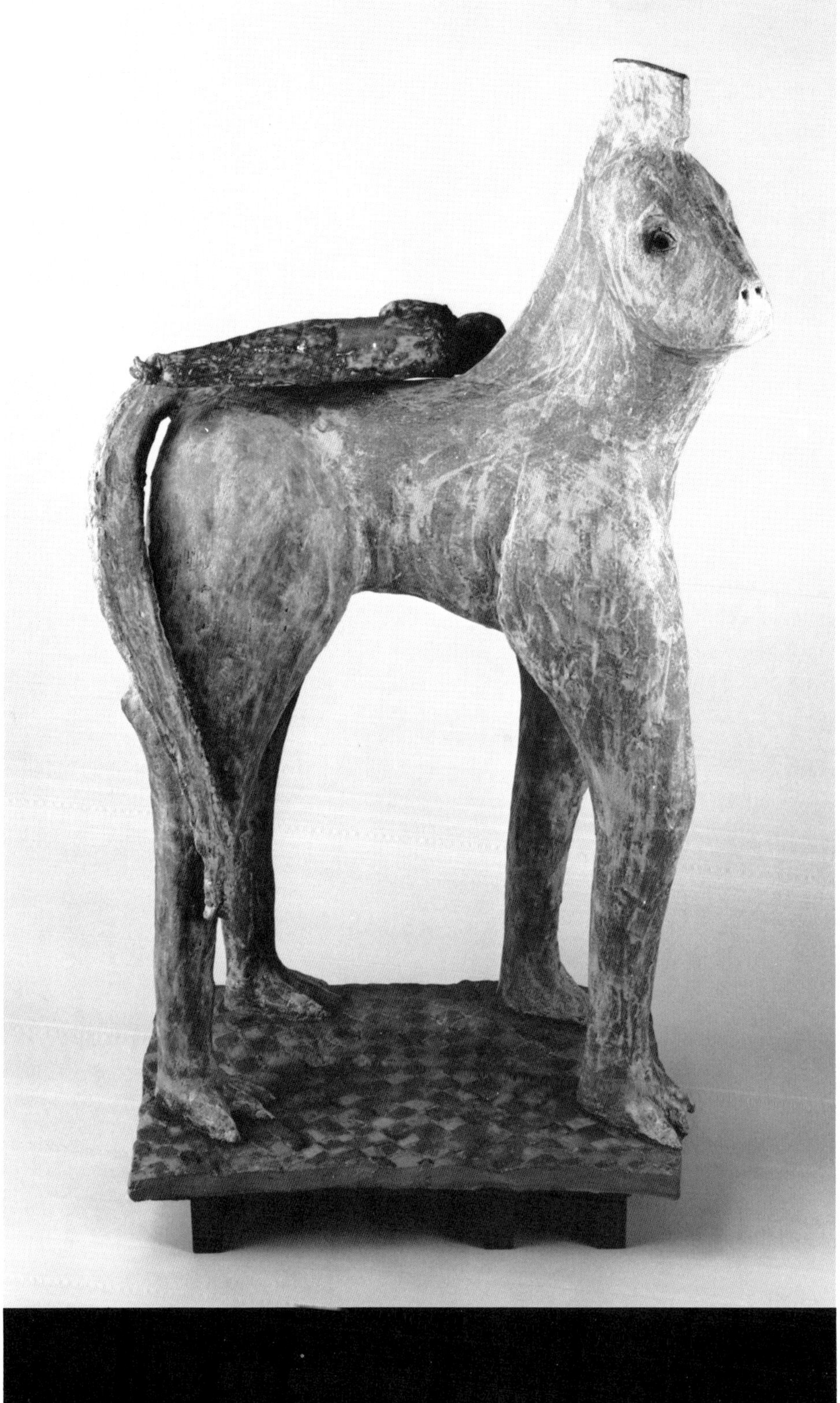

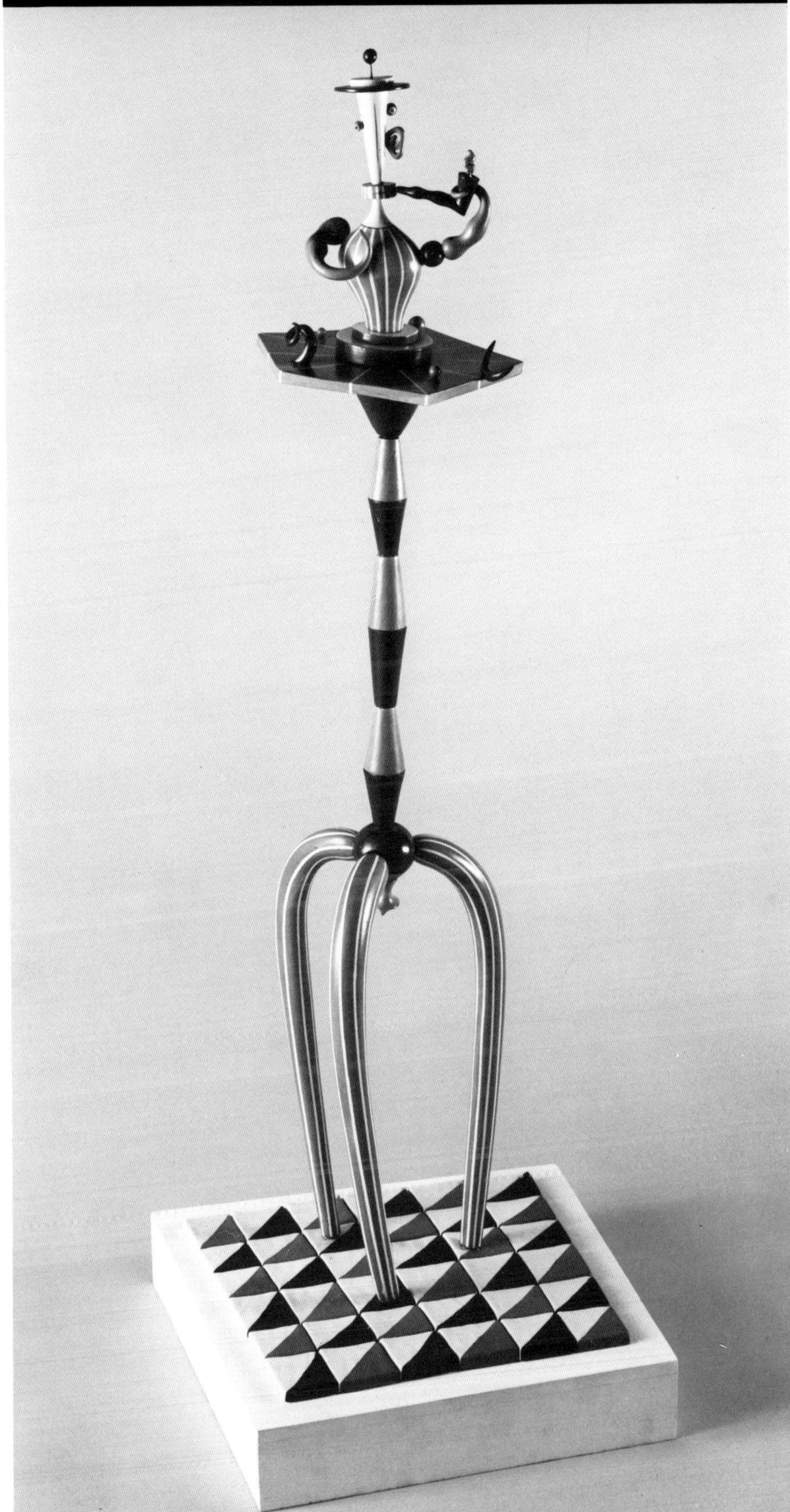

TOM RIPPON
The Smoker, 1986
porcelain
58 x 20½ x 19

CAROLYN RODKIN
Plaid and Lustre Plate, 1984
porcelain
2 x 12 diam.

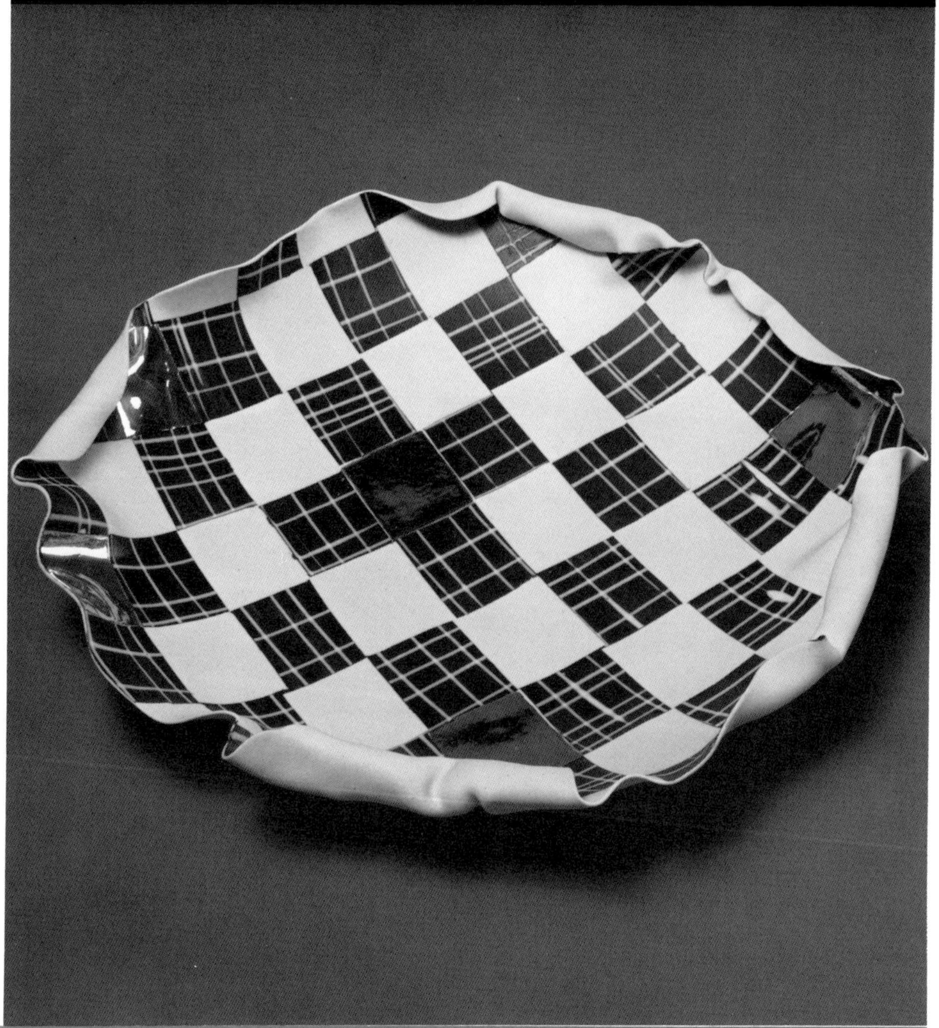

VIRGINIA SCOTCHIE
Mound, 1986
earthenware
84 x 48 x 24

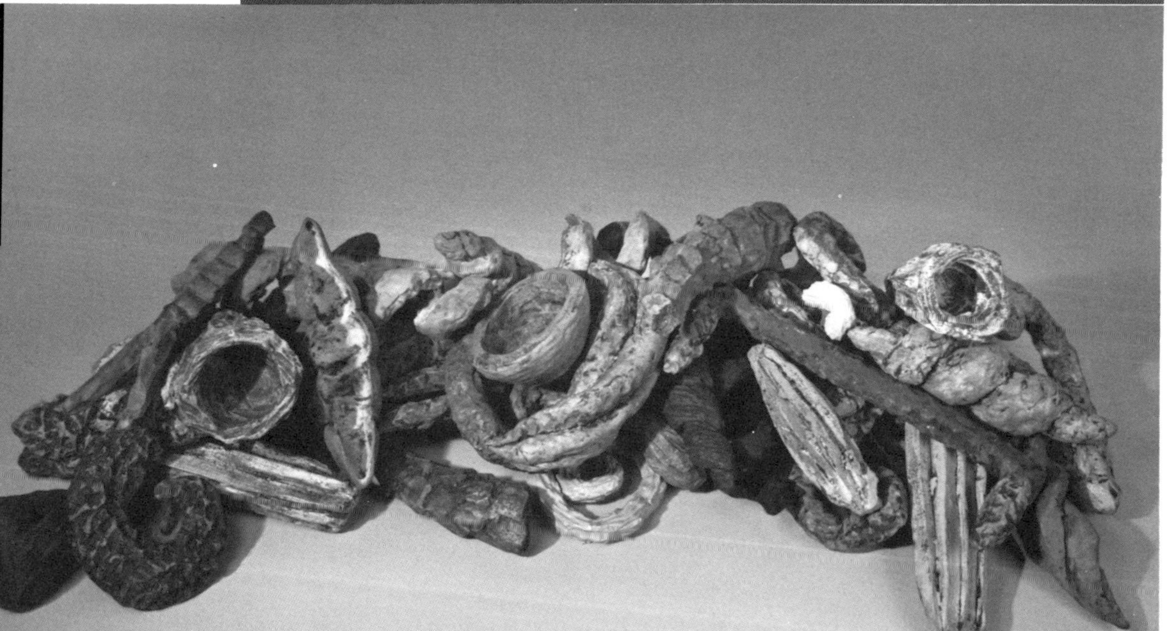

ARLENE SHECHET
Cella, 1986
earthenware
17 x 15 x 9

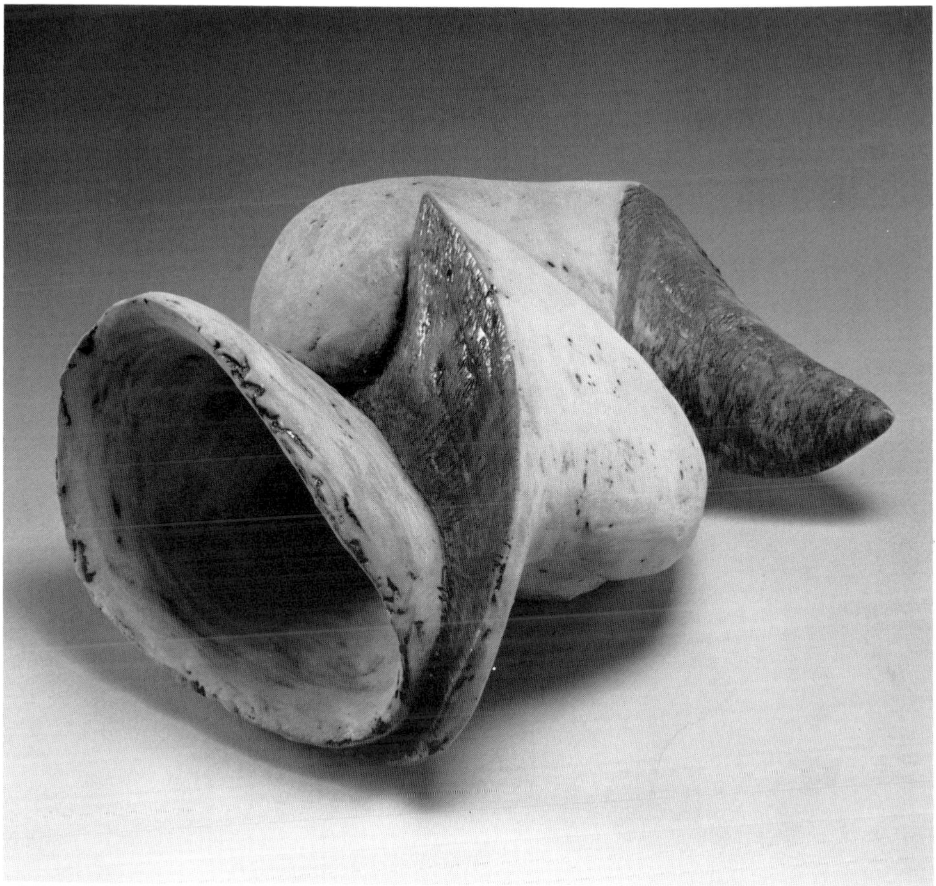

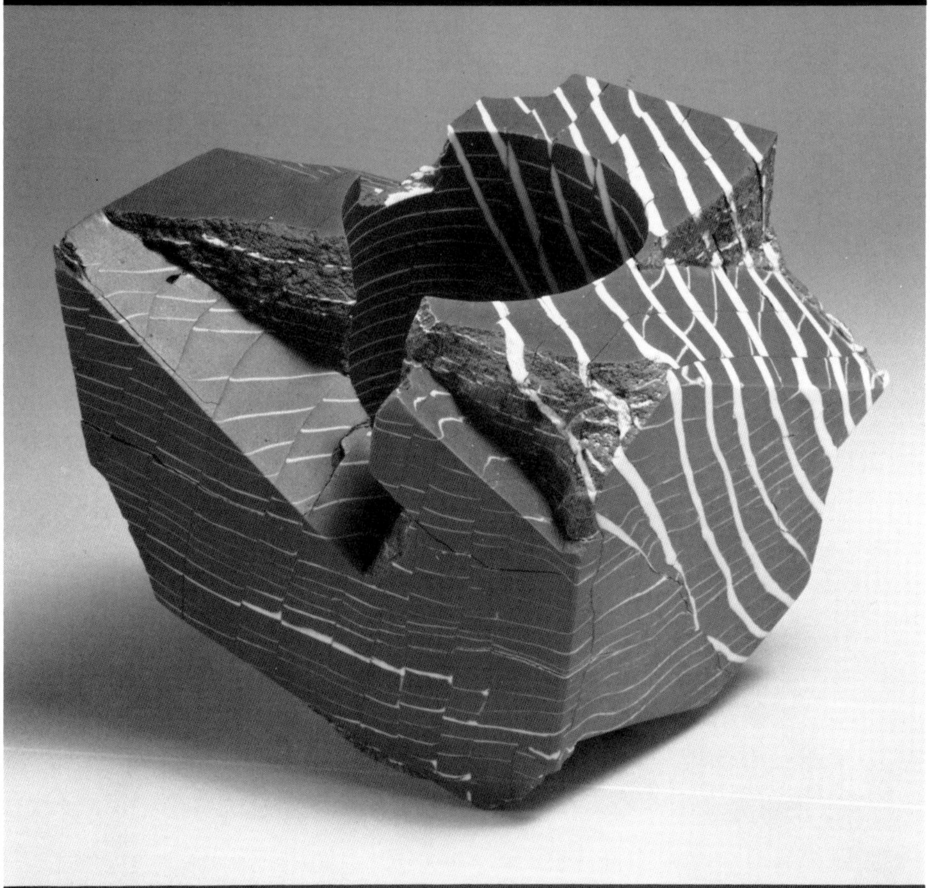

SALLY URBAN SILBERBERG
Ilissos, 1986
porcelain
10 x 6½ x 6¾

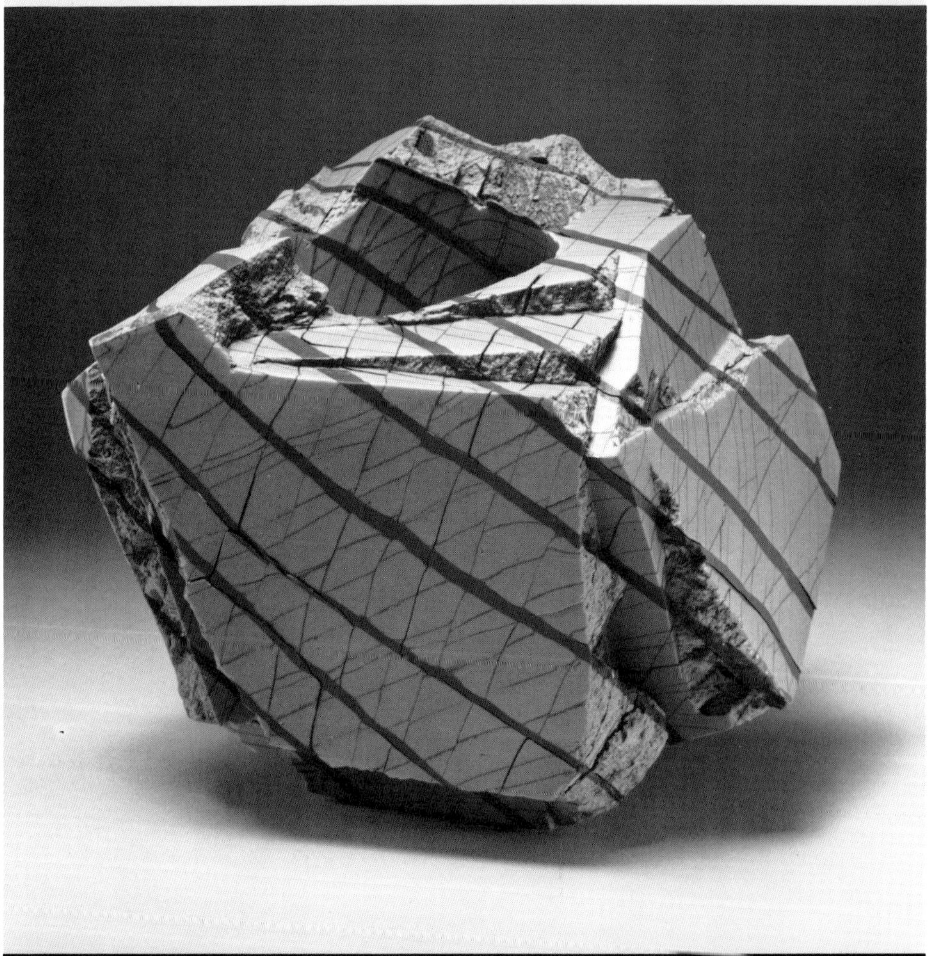

SALLY URBAN SILBERBERG
Ledges II, 1986
porcelain
8 x 6¼ x 6½

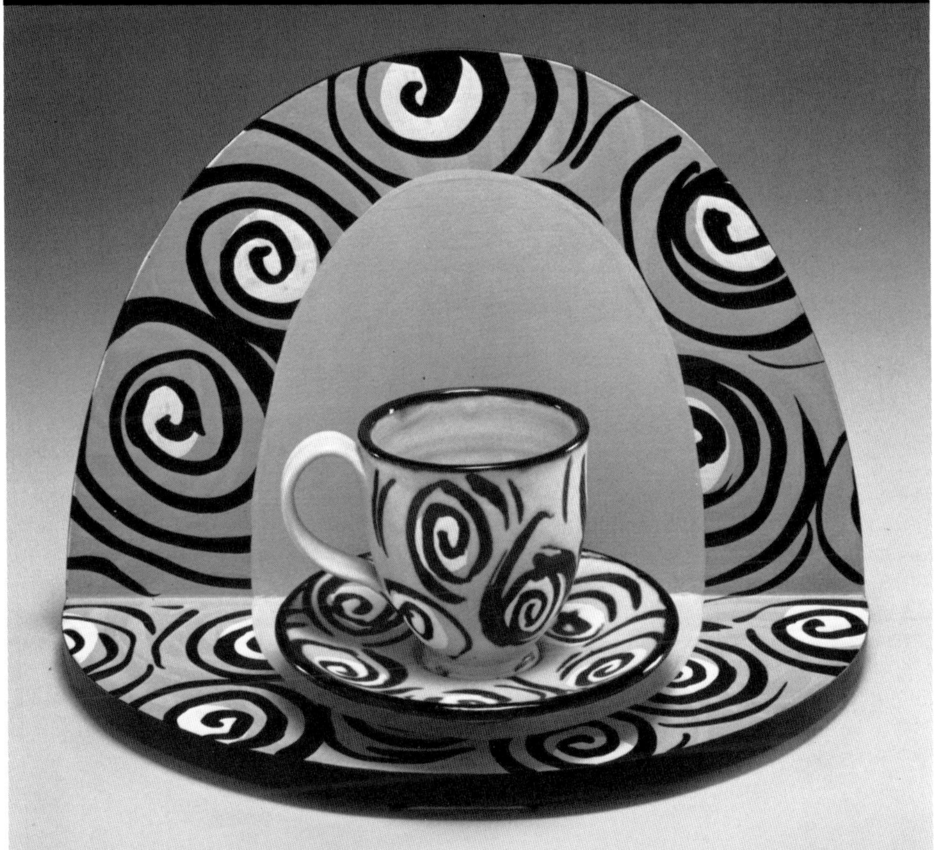

ANNE SMITH
Cup and Saucer with Shelf, 1986
porcelain and wood
Cup: 3¼ x 4⅜ diam.
Saucer: 1 x 5⅝ diam.
Shelf: 9 x 12 x 8

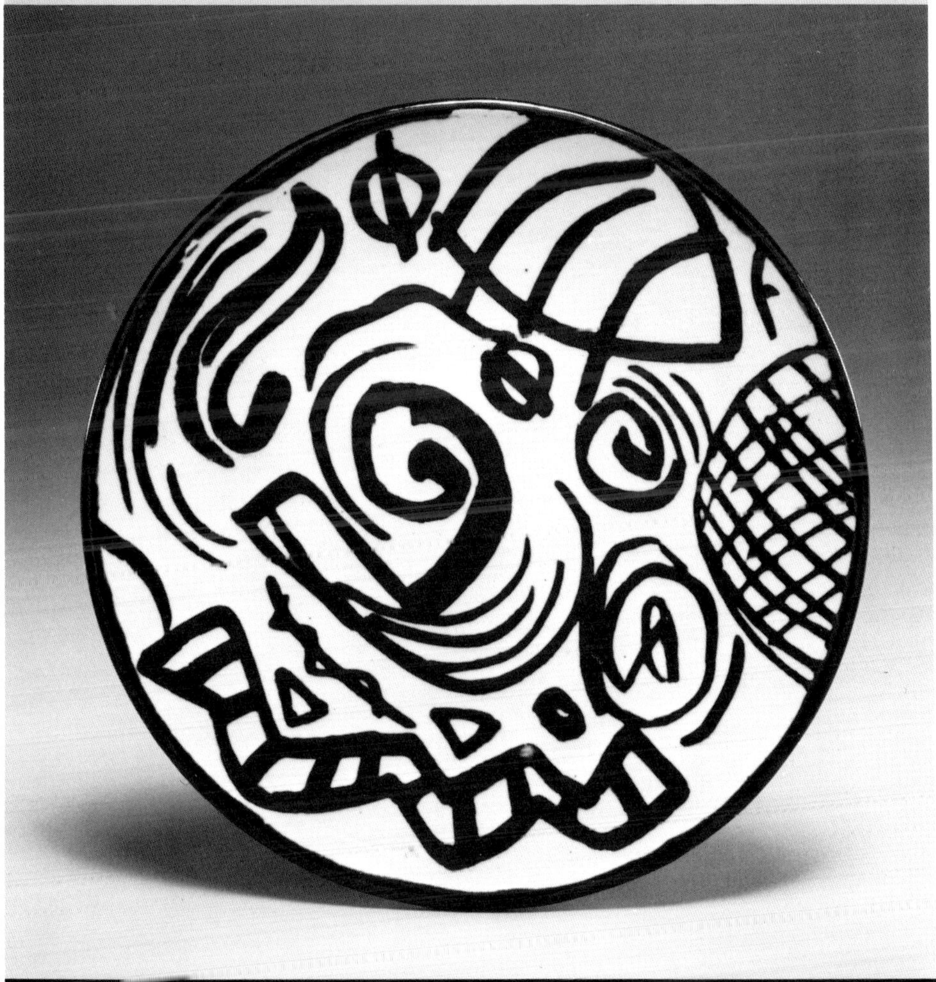

ANNE SMITH
Black and White Plate #1, 1986
porcelain
⅞ x 11 diam.

CHRIS STALEY
Vase, 1986
porcelain
20 x 7 diam.

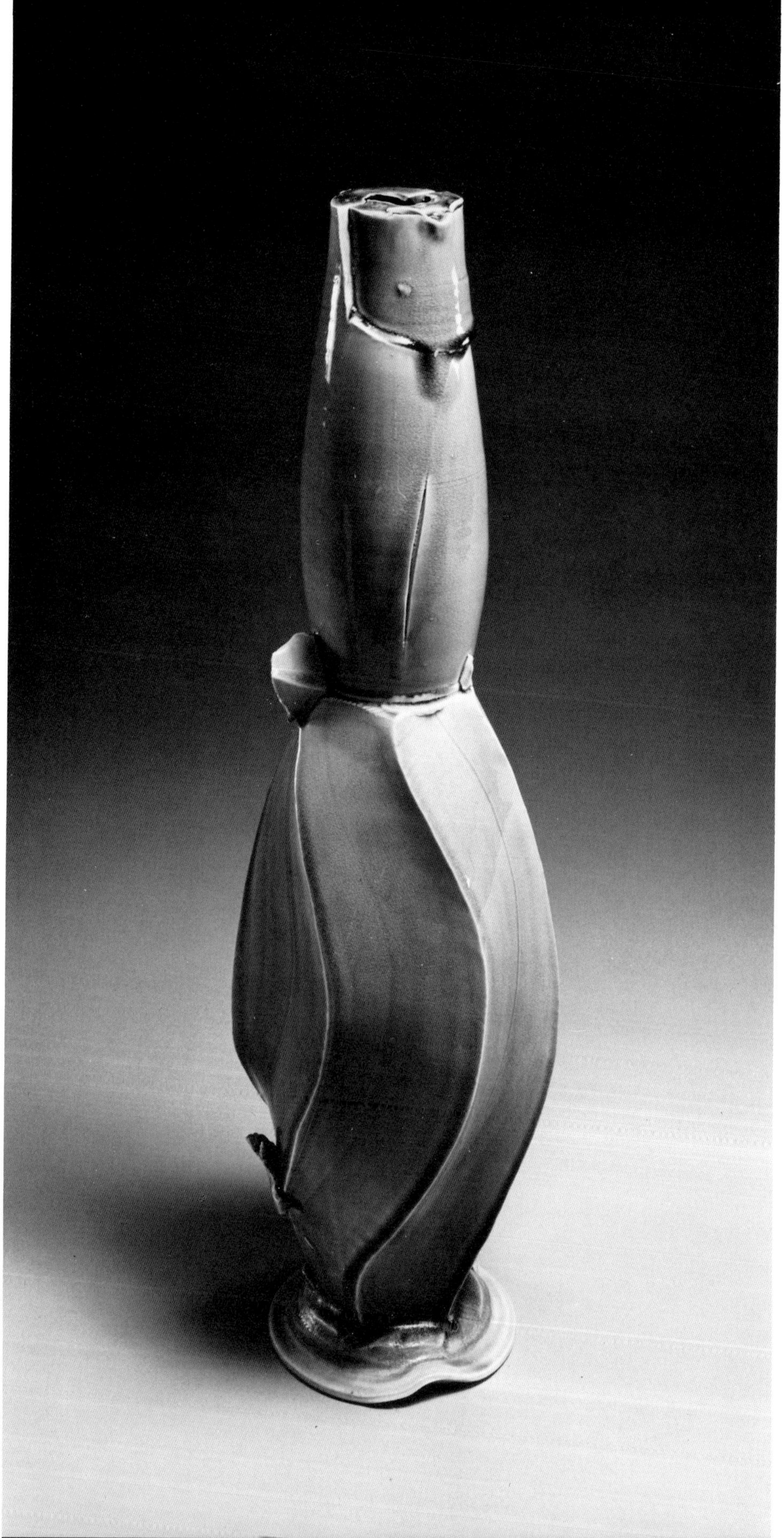

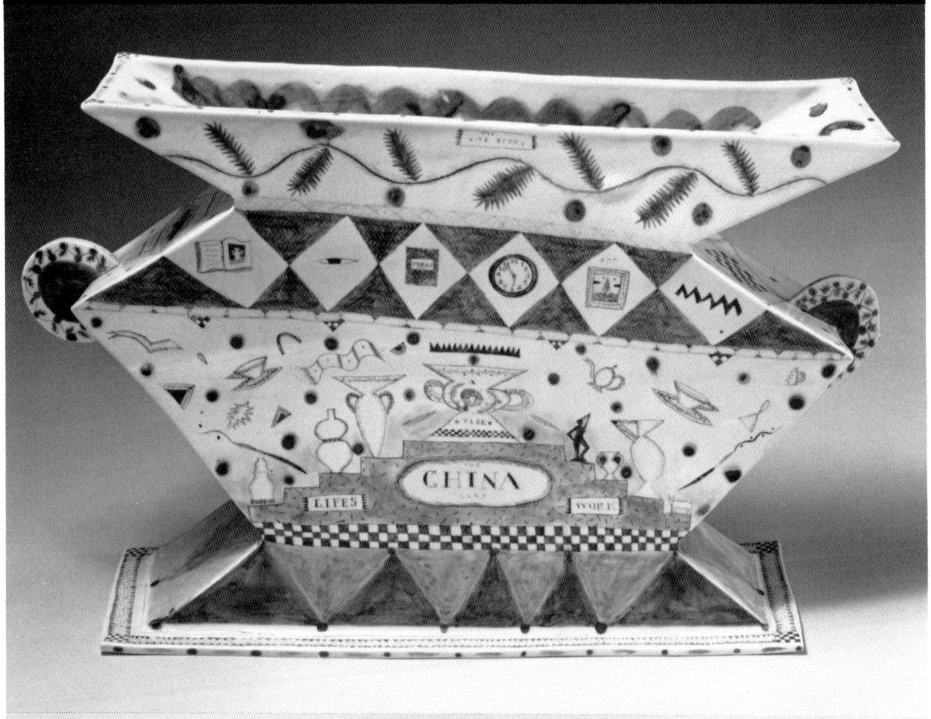

MARA SUPERIOR
China: A Life's Work
(side one),
The Homestead
(side two), 1985
porcelain
13 x 21 x 5

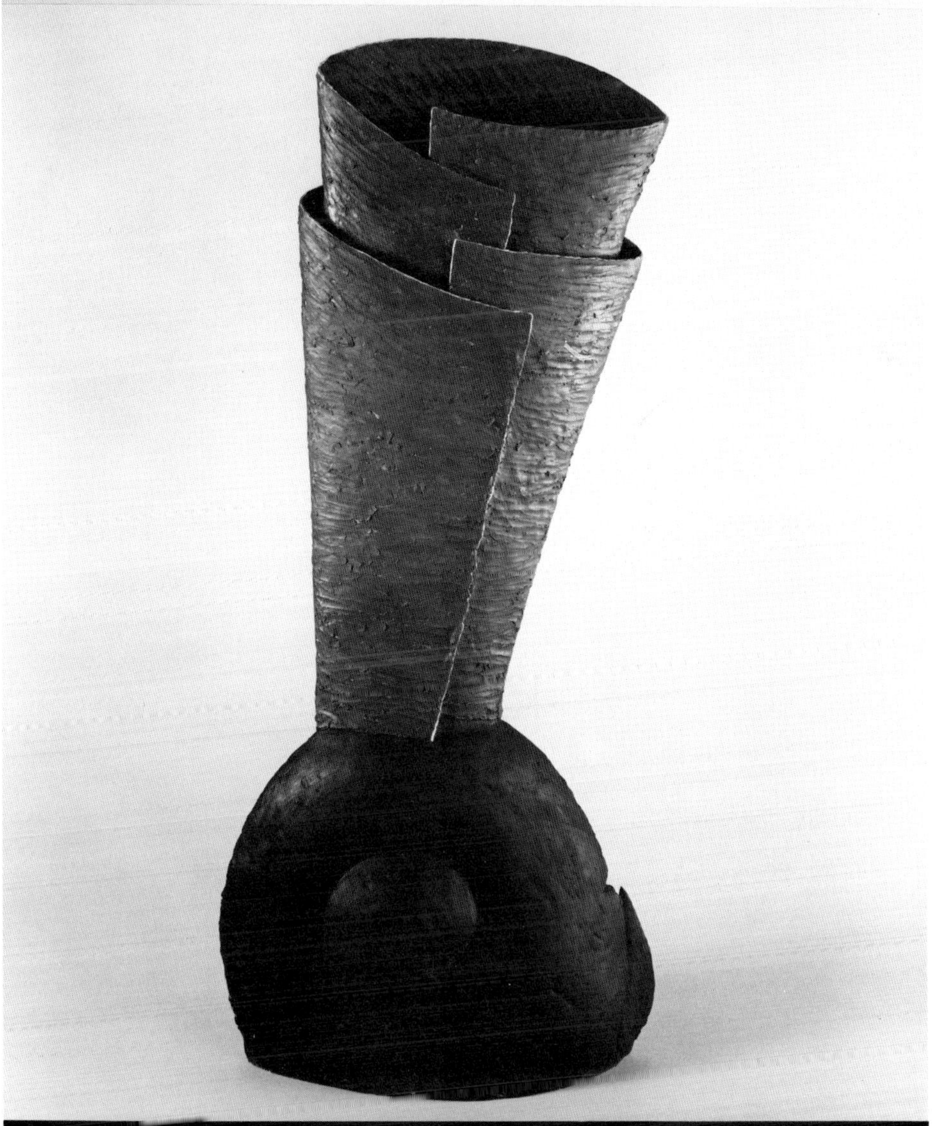

DENNIS TOBIN
Inherited Duality, 1986
earthenware
52 x 22 x 9

DONNA WEBB
Water Vase, 1986
stoneware
12 x 9 x 6

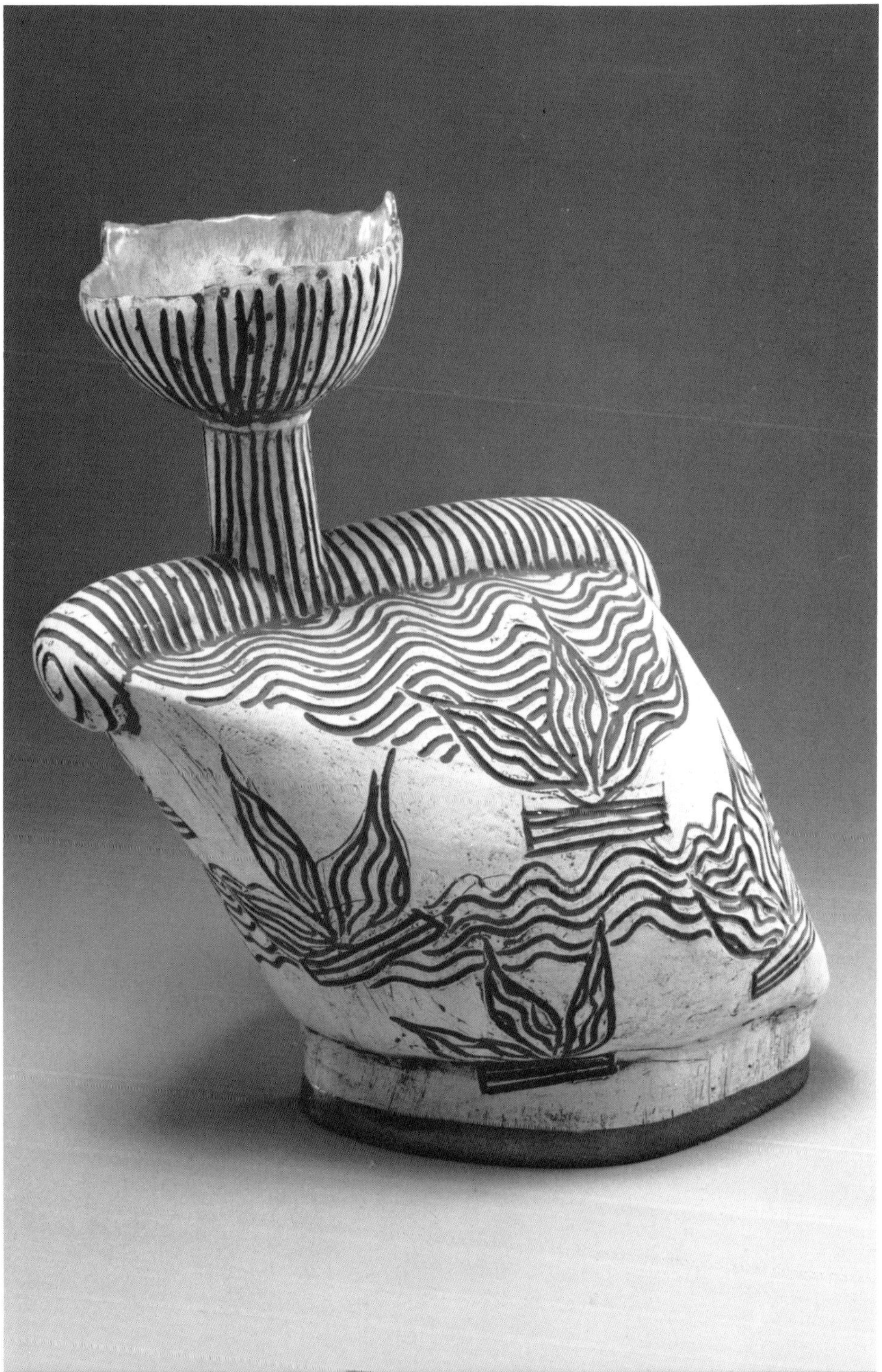

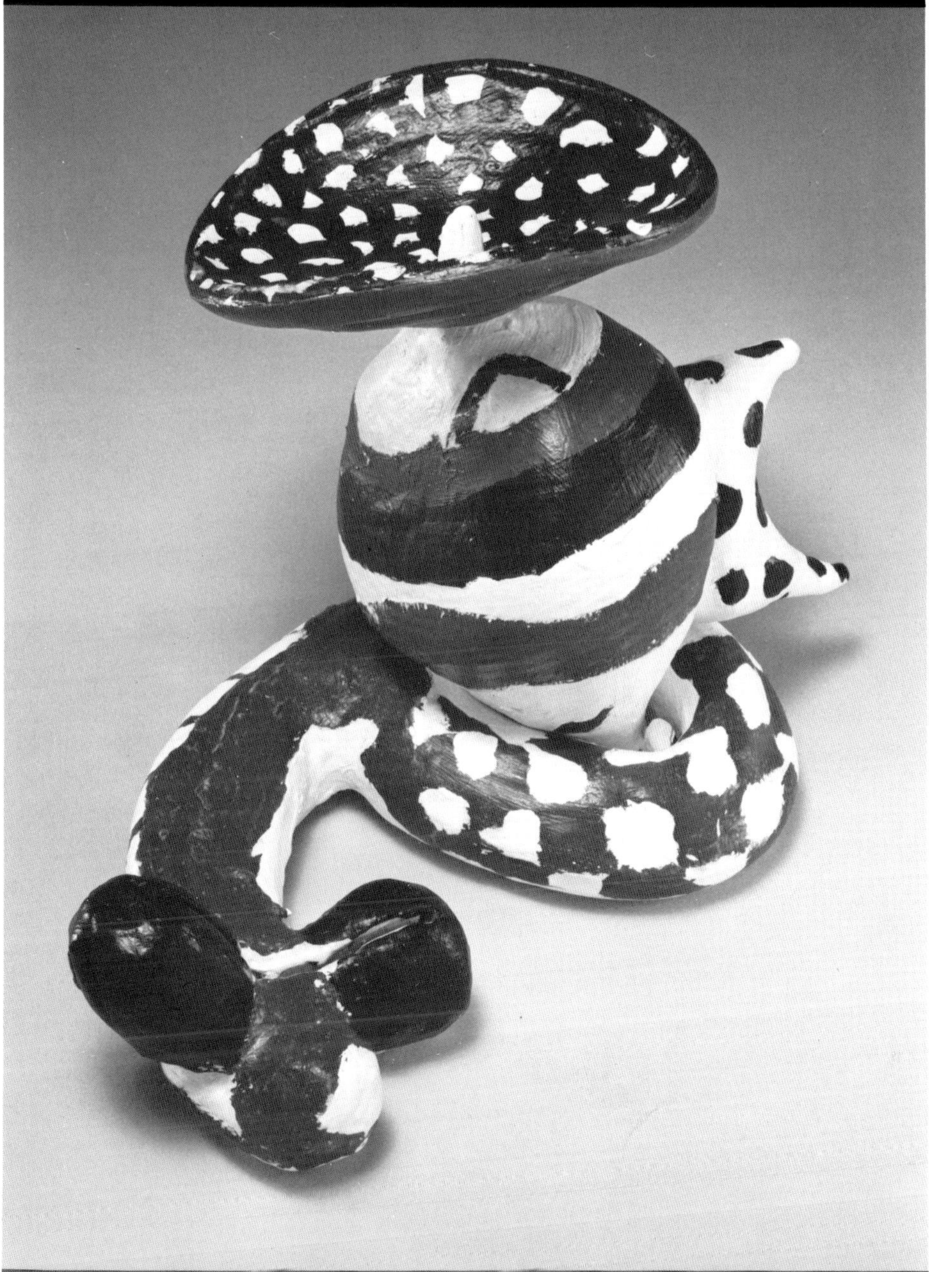

ANN WEBER
The Effects of Sociability on Sunday Dinner, 1986
earthenware
10 x 15 x 9

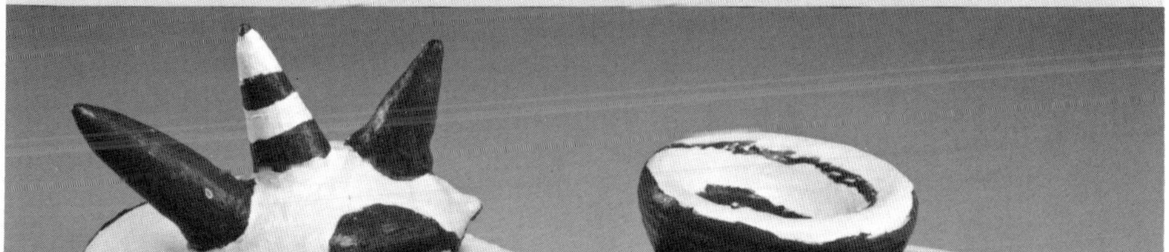

ANN WEBER
Gathering, Cultivating, Fishing, 1986
earthenware
8 x 18 x 10

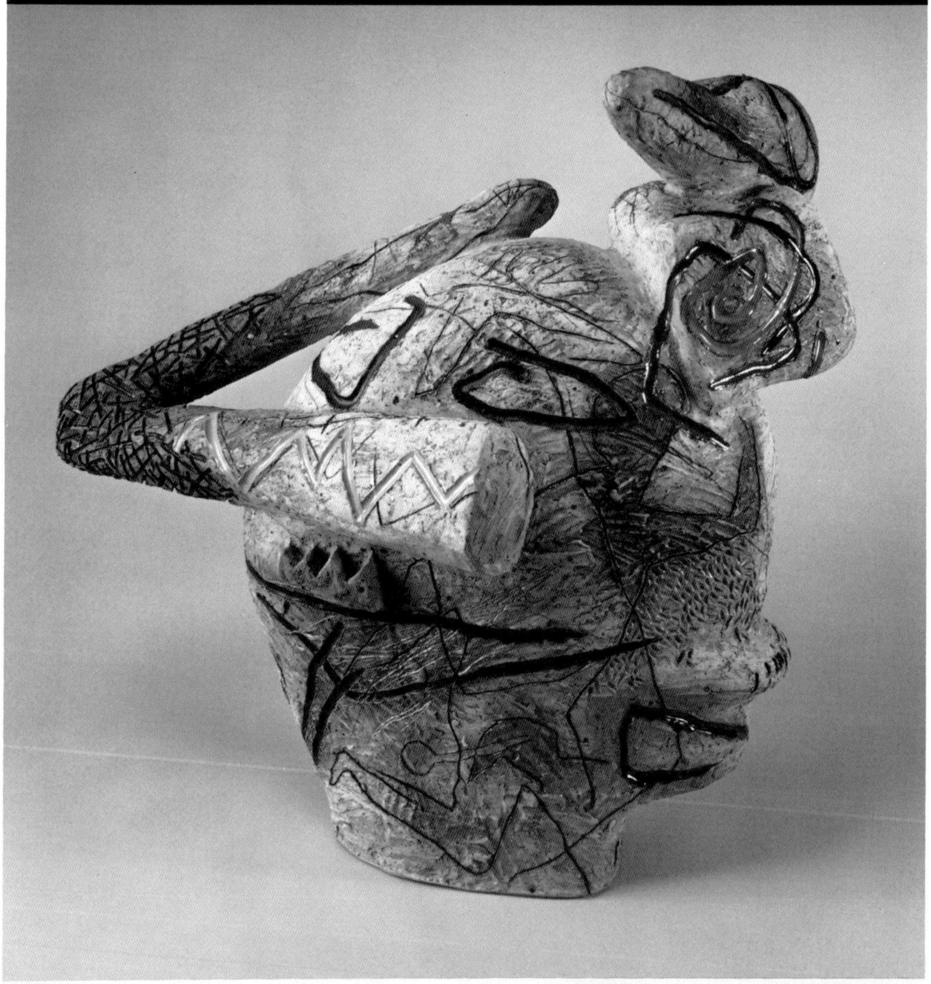

STANTON P. WELSH
Hollow Horn, 1986
earthenware
43¼ x 44 x 22

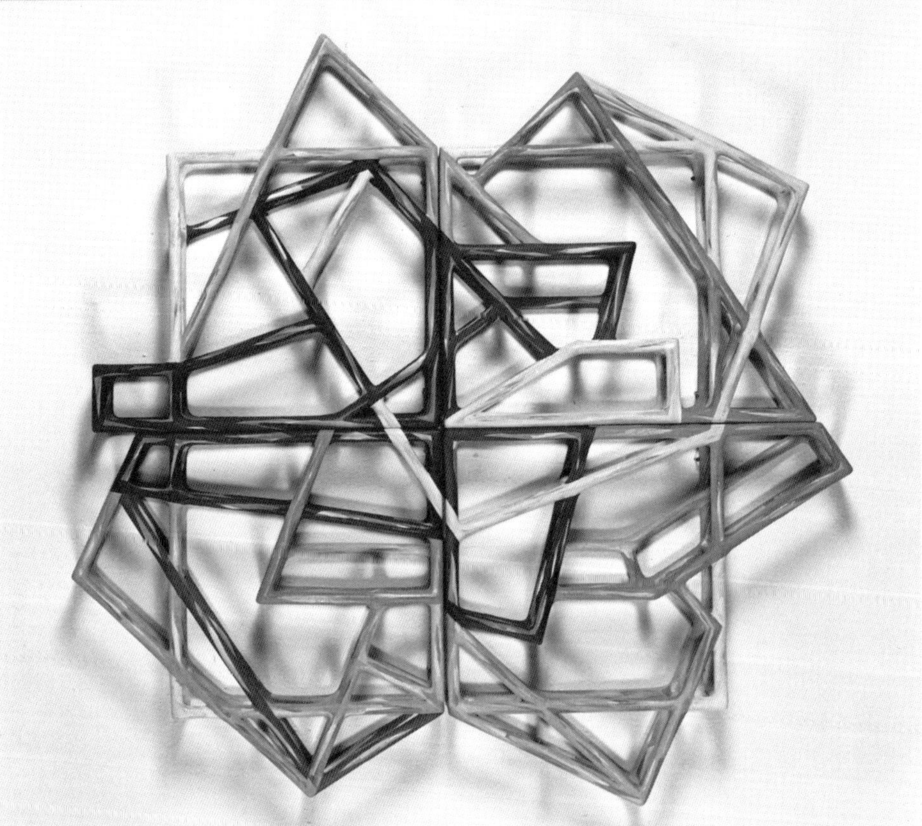

NICHOLAS WOOD
Houses in Motion #6,
1985
earthenware
54 x 52 x 6

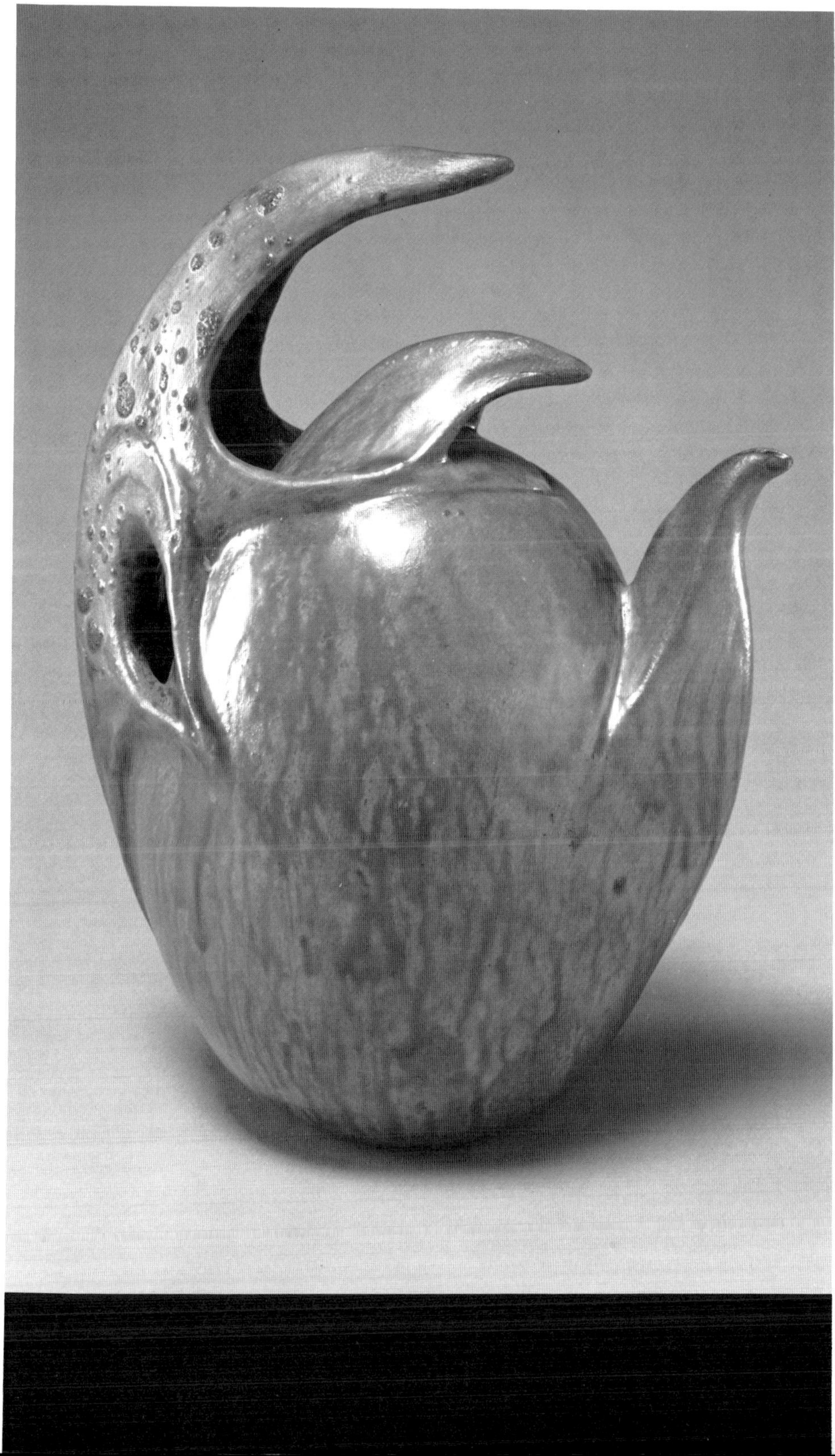

HEATHER YOUNG
?, 1986
earthenware
9 x 5 x 7

ARNOLD ZIMMERMAN
Untitled, 1986
stoneware
32 x 15 x 15

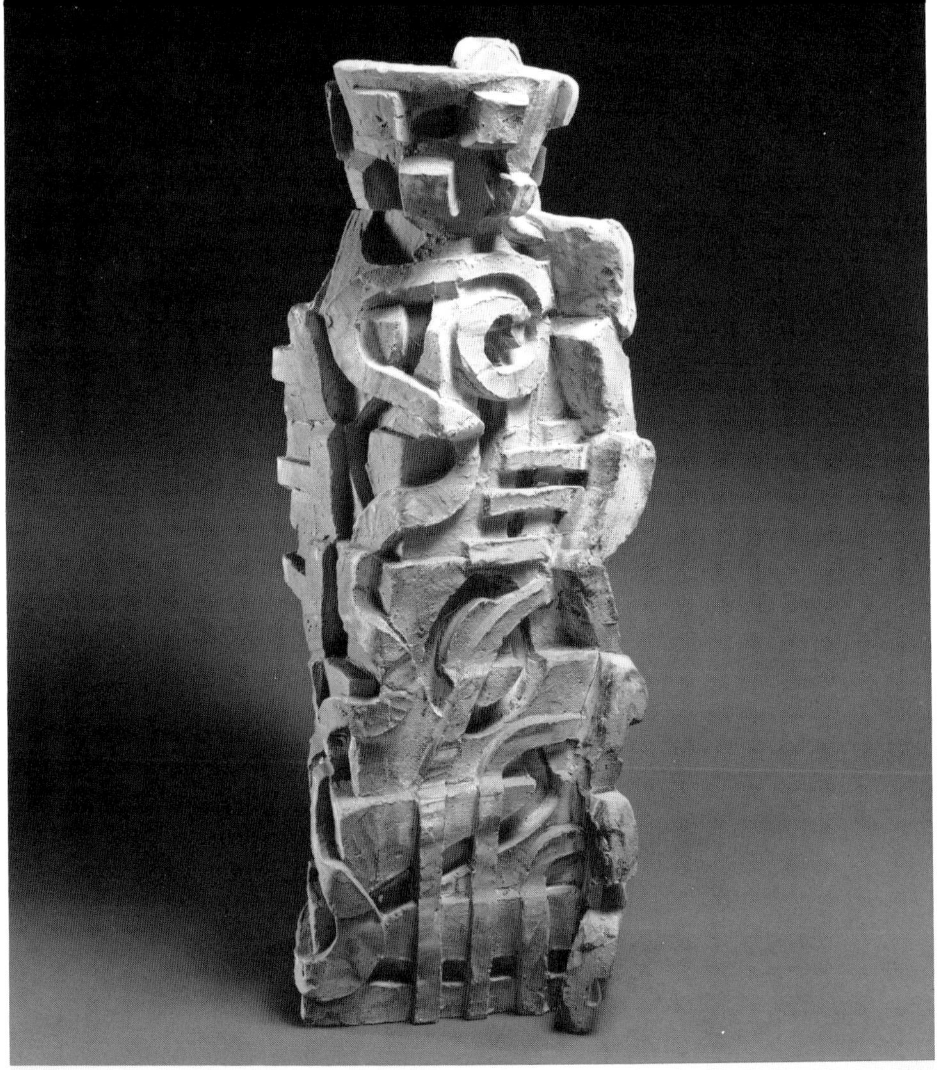

GEORGETTE ZIRBES
Souvenir Plate #13, 1986
stoneware
2½ x 20 diam.

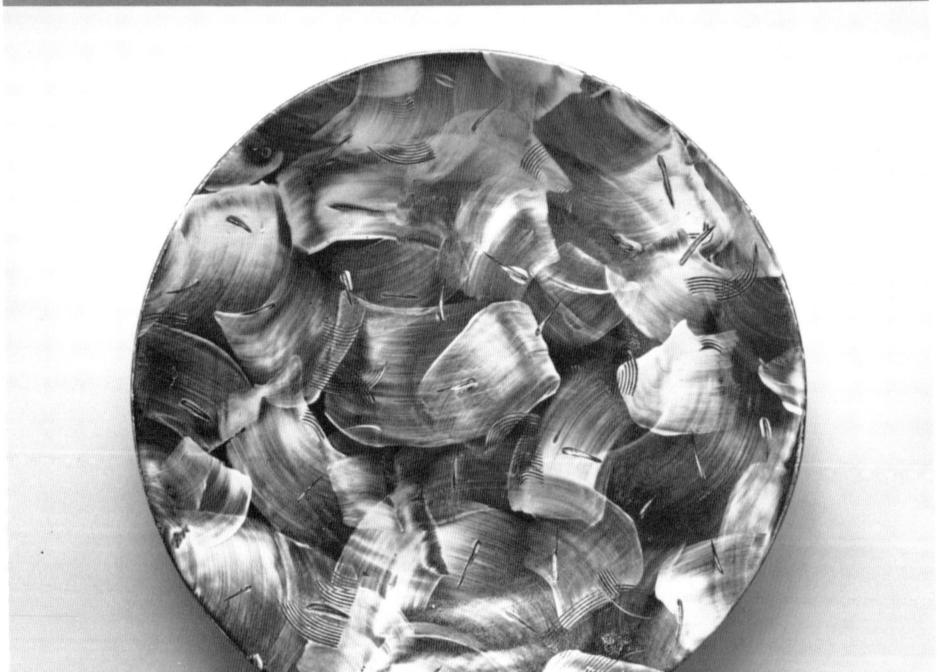

CHECKLIST OF THE EXHIBITION

All dimensions are given in inches and, unless otherwise noted, are listed in order of height, width, and depth.

INVITATIONAL

ROBERT ARNESON
Clay I Am, It Is True, 1982-83
stoneware
83 x 25 x 25
Courtesy Allan Frumkin Gallery, New York, NY

RUDY AUTIO
Goodbye to the Girls on Galena Street, 1986
stoneware
36 x 26 x 25
Courtesy of the artist

WILLIAM DALEY
Oval Chamber, 1986
stoneware
39½ x 18 x 23
Courtesy of the artist

STEPHEN DE STAEBLER
Standing Figure with Dark Aura, 1984
stoneware
99 x 18 x 21
Courtesy of CDS Gallery, New York, NY

RICHARD DE VORE
Pot #363, 1983
stoneware
6¾ x 15½ diam.
Courtesy Max Protetch Gallery, New York, NY

JACK EARL
He Looked and Found NOMAN, 1986
earthenware
28½ x 19 x 22¼
Courtesy Theo Portnoy Gallery, New York, NY

MARY FRANK
Lovers, 1983
earthenware
21½ x 21½ x 15
Courtesy Rena Bransten Gallery, San Francisco, CA

VIOLA FREY
Untitled (Man/Nude/Woman/Figurines), 1986
earthenware
39½ x 19½ x 16
Courtesy Rena Bransten Gallery, San Francisco, CA

WAYNE HIGBY
Mammoth Rock Beach, 1984
earthenware
10½ x 19 x 16
Courtesy of Donna Higby

JUN KANEKO
Untitled, 1986
stoneware
32 x 17 x 20
Courtesy of the artist

JOHN MASON
Untitled, 1984
stoneware
16 x 13 x 13
Courtesy of the artist

RON NAGLE
Orange Tracy, 1986
earthenware
3¼ x 4 x 1¾
Courtesy Charles Cowles Gallery, New York, NY

RON NAGLE
Black Knob Job, 1984
earthenware
3¼ x 4 x 1¾
Courtesy Rena Bransten Gallery, San Francisco, CA

KEN PRICE
Club Atomica, 1986
earthenware
15 x 9½ diam.
Collection Everson Museum of Art, Syracuse, NY

ADRIAN SAXE
Untitled Jar, 1985
porcelain and stoneware
13 x 9½ x 15½
Courtesy of the artist

RICHARD SHAW
Paper Lighthouse, 1985
porcelain
21 x 20 x 9
Courtesy Allan Frumkin Gallery, New York, NY

PAUL SOLDNER
Pedestal Piece, 1985
earthenware
30 x 32 x 7
Courtesy Scripps College, Claremont, CA, Collection of Fred and Estelle Marer

RUDOLF STAFFEL
Untitled, 1986
porcelain
7½ x 4½ x 4½
Courtesy Helen Drutt Gallery, Philadelphia, PA

PETER VOULKOS
Untitled, 1983
earthenware
10½ x 13½ x 10
Courtesy Charles Cowles Gallery, New York, NY

BETTY WOODMAN
Zante, 1985
earthenware
31 x 21 x 9
Courtesy Max Protetch Gallery, New York, NY

JURIED

BILL ABRIGHT, San Anselmo, CA
Rice Lady, 1986
stoneware, wood
22 x 10 x 13

NANCY ADAMS, San Geronimo, CA
Spirit Corn Vessel, 1986
earthenware
12 x 10 x 7½

DOROTHY BAKER, Snowmass Village, CO
Untitled, 1984
stoneware
12½ x 15 x 15

CURTIS AND SUZAN BENZLE, Columbus, OH
After You're Gone, 1986
porcelain
7 x 17 x 3

NINA BORGIA-ABERLE, Johnstown, OH
Two Tops, 1986
earthenware
18 x 18 x 5

TOBY BUONAGURIO, Bronx, NY
Streamline Robot, 1985
earthenware
23 x 15 x 12
Courtesy Bernice Steinbaum Gallery, New York, NY

MARK BURNS, Philadelphia, PA
Vice Squad, 1985
earthenware, wood, wire, paint
40 x 22 x 36

JIM CASWELL, Santa Monica, CA
Ma Tante Pandore, 1986
earthenware
10 x 15 x 24

BETH CHANGSTROM, Penngrove, CA
Blackie Turns Green, 1986
earthenware
28 x 28 x 2
Collection Ruth Summers and Bruce Bowen

SCOTT CHAMBERLIN, Boulder, CO
Untitled, 1986
earthenware
84 x 60 x 22

PATRICK S. CRABB, Tustin, CA
Relic Dispenser, 1986
earthenware, metal
16½ x 10½ x 10½

ANNE CURRIER, Alfred, NY
Réciproque, 1986
earthenware
29 x 22 x 9

ROSELINE DELISLE, Venice, CA
Triptyque 6, 1986
porcelain
21 x 6¾ diam.

MARK DERBY, Long Beach, CA
Blue Vase, 1986
stoneware
20 x 6 x 9

STEVEN DONEGAN, Philadelphia, PA
Break with Tradition, 1986
earthenware
43½ x 44½ x 7

PAUL A. DRESANG, Edwardsville, IL
Untitled, 1986
porcelain
7 x 8 x 4

GARY ERICKSON, Rush City, MN
Stout Blue Spiral, 1986
earthenware
38 x 24 x 24

RON FONDAW, Miami, FL
Birth Cone, 1985
porcelain
27 x 20 x 13

JOHN FRANTZ, Fries, VA
Untitled, 1986
earthenware
25 x 25 x 6

BELINDA GABRYL, Providence, RI
Tornado Teapot and Creamer, 1986
earthenware
Teapot: 11¼ x 10½ x 9
Creamer: 5¼ x 4½ x 3¾

CLIFF GARTEN, St. Paul, MN
Hatch, Hatch, 1984
earthenware
67½ x 41½ x 10¼

ANNE GOLDMAN, Walnut Creek, CA
Stone Flower Vase, 1986
stoneware
14 x 18 diam.

MICHAEL GUBKIN, Cleveland Heights, OH
An Insatiate Ingrate, 1986
stoneware
30 x 14½ diam.

CHRIS GUSTIN,
South Dartmouth, MA
Vase, 1986
stoneware
21 x 11 x 10

DOROTHY HAFNER,
New York, NY
Gazpacho Server II, 1986
porcelain
Server: 8 x 11½ x 11½
Ladle: 11 long

WALTER HALL, Simsbury, CT
Incident at Sea, 1986
earthenware, steel
24 x 21 x 13

RICHARD HIRSCH,
West Newbury, MA
Ceremonial Cup #26,
1985-86
stoneware
12 x 12½ x 12

ABBY HUNTOON,
Portland, ME
Black Vase with Pedestal,
1985
earthenware
50 x 18 x 19

ITSUE ITO, Minneapolis, MN
Shutoh, 1986
earthenware
16 x 16 x 14

MARK D. JOHNSON,
Hartford, CT
Vase, 1986
stoneware
20 x 9 diam.

JAMES KLUEG, Duluth, MN
Arbor, 1986
earthenware
13 x 18 x 8

JAMES LAWTON, Alfred, NY
Teapot with Overcoat, 1985
earthenware
10 x 10 x 4

PATRICK LOUGHRAN,
New York, NY
Untitled Plate, 1986
earthenware
3½ x 24 diam.

JOE MARISCAL,
Stockton, CA
Doing a Nickel and Change, 1984
earthenware
23 x 16 x 12

PAUL MATHIEU, Venice, CA
The Order of Desires, 1986
porcelain
12¾ x 12¾ x 4¼

JUANITA JIMENEZ MIZUNO,
Los Angeles, CA
Hittite Series #9, 1985
earthenware
24 x 36 x 5

JUDY MOONELIS,
New York, NY
Woman in Bed II, 1986
earthenware
16 x 27 x 13

JUDY MOONELIS,
New York, NY
Curving Head, 1984-85
earthenware
44 x 45 x 22

JANET NEUWALDER,
Jamaica Plains, MA
Teapot, 1985
porcelain
13 x 20 x 12

RICHARD T. NOTKIN,
Myrtle Point, OR
Cube Skull Teapot (Variation #6), Yixing Series, 1985
stoneware
5¼ x 6 x 2¾

FRANK OZEREKO,
Pelham, MA
Interior 6, 1986
earthenware
36 x 30 x 21
Collection of Meredyth and John Moses

MARIO PETRIRENA,
Decatur, GA
Black Madonnas Are Never Wasted on Benjamin Jones, 1986
earthenware
23 x 19 x 7

PATRICIA RIEGER,
Chapel Hill, NC
Sentinel, 1986
earthenware
60 x 38 x 21

TOM RIPPON, Cookeville, TN
The Smoker, 1986
porcelain
58 x 20½ x 19

CAROLYN RODKIN,
Oakland, CA
Plaid and Lustre Plate, 1984
porcelain
2 x 12 diam.

VIRGINIA SCOTCHIE,
Morgantown, WV
Mound, 1986
earthenware
84 x 48 x 24

ARLENE SHECHET,
New York, NY
Cella, 1986
earthenware
17 x 15 x 9

SALLY URBAN SILBERBERG,
Plainfield, MA
Ilissos, 1986
porcelain
10 x 6½ x 6¾

SALLY URBAN SILBERBERG,
Plainfield, MA
Ledges II, 1986
porcelain
8 x 6¼ x 6½

ANNE SMITH, Somerville, MA
Black and White Plate #1,
1986
porcelain
⅞ x 11 diam.

ANNE SMITH, Somerville, MA
Cup and Saucer with Shelf,
1986
porcelain and wood
Cup: 3¼ x 4⅜ diam.
Saucer: 1 x 5⅝ diam.
Shelf: 9 x 12 x 8

CHRIS STALEY, Wichita, KS
Vase, 1986
porcelain
20 x 7 diam.

MARA SUPERIOR,
Williamsburg, MA
China: A Life's Work (side one), **The Homestead** (side two), 1985
porcelain
13 x 21 x 5

DENNIS TOBIN,
Bloomington, IL
Inherited Duality, 1986
earthenware
52 x 22 x 9

DONNA WEBB, Akron, OH
Water Vase, 1986
stoneware
12 x 9 x 6

ANN WEBER, Canyon, CA
The Effects of Sociability on Sunday Dinner, 1986
earthenware
10 x 15 x 9

ANN WEBER, Canyon, CA
Gathering, Cultivating, Fishing, 1986
earthenware
8 x 18 x 10

STANTON P. WELSH,
Oakland, CA
Hollow Horn, 1986
earthenware
43¼ x 44 x 22
Courtesy Esther Saks Gallery
Chicago, IL

NICHOLAS WOOD,
Arlington, TX
Houses in Motion #6, 1985
earthenware
54 x 52 x 6

HEATHER YOUNG, Ojai, CA
?, 1986
earthenware
9 x 5 x 7

ARNOLD ZIMMERMAN,
New York, NY
Untitled, 1986
stoneware
32 x 15 x 15

GEORGETTE ZIRBES,
Ann Arbor, MI
Souvenir Plate #13, 1986
stoneware
2½ x 20 diam.